D1502349

FEEDBACK AND ORGANIZATION DEVELOPMENT: USING DATA-BASED METHODS

FEEDBACK AND ORGANIZATION DEVELOPMENT: USING DATA-BASED METHODS

DAVID A. NADLER

Columbia University

ADDISON-WESLEY PUBLISHING COMPANY
Reading, Massachusetts • Menlo Park, California
London • Amsterdam • Don Mills, Ontario • Sydney

This book is in the Addison-Wesley series:

ORGANIZATION DEVELOPMENT

Consulting Editors
Edgar H. Schein
Richard Beckhard
Warren G. Bennis

ISBN 0-201-05006-4
ABCDEFGHIJ-HC-7987

G93-378WLe

for my parents,
Leonard and Zeace Nadler

FOREWORD

It has been five years since the Addison-Wesley series on organization development published the books by Roeber, Galbraith, and Steele, and it is almost ten years since the series itself was launched in an effort to define the then-emerging field of organization development. Almost from its inception the series enjoyed a great success and helped to define what was then only a budding field of inquiry. Much has happened in the last ten years. There are now dozens of textbooks and readers on OD; research results are beginning to accumulate on what kinds of OD approaches have what effects; educational programs on planned change and OD are growing; and there are regional, national, and even international associations of practitioners of planned change and OD. All of these trends suggest that this area of practice has taken hold and found an important niche for itself in the applied social sciences and that its intellectual underpinnings are increasingly solidifying.

One of the most important trends we have observed in the last five years is the connecting of the field of planned change and OD to the mainstream of organization theory, organizational psychology, and organizational sociology. Although the field has its roots primarily in these underlying disciplines, it is only in recent years that basic textbooks in "organization behavior" have begun routinely referring to organization development as an applied area that students and managers alike must be aware of.

The editors of this series have attempted to keep an open mind on the question of when the series has fulfilled its function and should be allowed to die. The series should be kept alive only as long as new areas of knowledge and practice central to organization development are emerging. During the last year or so, several such areas have been defined, leading to the decision to continue the series.

On the applied side, it is clear that information is a basic nutrient for any kind of valid change process. Hence, a book on data gathering, surveys, and feedback methods is very timely. Nadler has done an especially important service in this area in focusing on the variety of methods which can be used in gathering information and feeding it back to clients. The book is eclectic in its approach, reflecting the fact that there are many ways to gather information, many kinds to be gathered, and many approaches to the feedback process to reflect the particular goals of the change program.

Team building and the appropriate use of groups continues to be a second key ingredient of most change programs. So far no single book in the field has dealt explicitly enough with this important process. Dyer's approach will help the manager to diagnose when to use and not use groups and, most important, how to carry out team building when that kind of intervention is appropriate.

One of the most important new developments in the area of planned change is the conceptualizing of how to work with large systems to initiate and sustain change over time. The key to this success is "transition management," a stage or process frequently referred to in change theories, but never explored systematically from both a theoretical and practical point of view. Beckhard and Harris present a model which will help the manager to think about this crucial area. In addition, they provide a set of diagnostic and action tools which will enable the change manager in large systems to get a concrete handle on transition management.

The area of organization design has grown in importance as organizations have become more complex. Davis and Lawrence provide a concise and definitive analysis of that particularly elusive organization design—the matrix organization—and elucidate clearly its forms, functions, and modes of operation.

Future volumes in the new series will explore the interconnections between OD and related areas which are becoming increasingly important to our total understanding of organizations, the process of management, and the nature of work. The whole quality-of-work-life area has spawned a growing concern with the nature of work itself and the context within which it occurs. Human-resource planning and career development are increasingly becoming organically linked to planned change programs. As people are discovering the variety of goals and aspirations which encompass different careers and life stages, more emphasis will have to be given to alternative work patterns and reward systems. All of these issues become even more complex in the multinational organization.

It is exciting to see our field develop, expand, strengthen its roots, and grow outward in many new directions. I believe that the core theory or the integrative framework is not yet at hand, but that the varied activities of the theoreticians, researchers, and practitioners of planned change and OD are increasingly relevant not only to the change manager, but also to line managers at all levels. As the recognition grows that part of *every* manager's job is to plan, initiate, and manage change, so will the relevance of concepts and methods in this area come to be seen as integral to the management process itself. It continues to be the goal of this series to provide such relevant concepts and methods to managers. I hope we have succeeded in some measure in this new series of books.

Cambridge, Massachusetts   Edgar H. Schein
June 1977

PREFACE

This book is about the use of data as a tool for organizational change. It attempts to bring together some of what we know from experience and research and to translate that knowledge into useful insights for those people who are thinking about using data-based methods in organizations. The need for such a book is based on my observation that the collection, interpretation, and feedback of data are very basic core activities that are present in almost all organization development (OD) interventions. Anyone working to help an organization grow, develop, and learn must collect and interpret data, and, in some way, must present the data to the people in the organization. The procedures may vary from the very structured questionnaires of survey feedback in large organizations to the less formal data collection of a process consultant working with a small group. What they have in common, however, is a set of activities involving the use of information.

Despite the pervasive use of data, only a few extensive pieces have been written about the use of data as a tool for working with organizations. The work that has been done has emphasized either one theory or set of procedures for using data. This book approaches the subject in a broader way—that is, it attempts to deal with a whole range of questions and issues concerning the various uses of data as an organizational-change tool.

Because different people have varying degrees of interest in the use of data-based methods, different strategies should be employed for reading this book. The book is divided into four parts. Part 1 answers the question "What does information as an organizational-change tool mean?" It contains information on the meaning, dimensions, and uses of data in organizations, provides case examples of data-based methods, and outlines a basic framework for thinking about data-based organizational change. Part 2 explains "why it works." This part outlines a theory of information and behavior, which explains why data have the potential to change behavior in organizations. Part 3 focuses on "how to use data?" Explanations of how to plan for data use, how to collect data, and how to feed back data are given. This part is supplemented by short appendixes on data analysis and data collection instruments. Part 4 gives some conclusions and indicates new directions for work.

Those who have only a general interest in understanding what data-based methods are should concentrate on Part 1 which is a self-contained unit and provides an introduction to the use of data as a change tool. For those who want to proceed a bit farther, Chapters 5 (Planning to use data), 6 (The process of collecting data), 8 (Feeding back data), and 9 (Perspectives and new directions) are recommended. Those who are considering the use of data-based methods, either as consultants or clients, should read the entire book.

The book is primarily addressed to people who want to learn more about OD; however, there are other possible audiences. In particular, people who do field research in organizational settings may find the material on data collection useful. Included are discussions of the problems that are encountered whenever one enters an organization to collect data, even if the data are merely for research purposes. The argument is made that data collection is not a benign act; indeed data collection is an intervention into organizational life. Thus organizational researchers and students planning to collect data in organizations may want to study Chapters 4, 5, and 6 in some detail.

The ideas presented are the result of several years of work with organizations and much thought about the use of information for organizational change. During that time I have been privileged to work with a number of people who have helped me immensely. While there are many I could name, I would like to acknowledge a few who have been particularly helpful in the work that led to this book. Three individuals who greatly aided my development as a student of organizations are Edward E. Lawler III, Harry Levinson, and Cortlandt Cammann. In addition a number of people have aided me in the development of my ideas about feedback and specifically in the writing of this book; they include Philip Mirvis, Jay Nisberg, and Rob Cooke. Edgar Schein, editor of this series, was extremely helpful in giving detailed feedback on draft chapters. A special thanks goes to my friend and colleague at Columbia, Michael Tushman, who served in the dual role of critic and supporter.

Several organizations have also been instrumental in the development of this book. My ideas reflect the time that I spent on the staff of the Survey Research Center of the Institute for Social Research at the University of Michigan. The Institute provided a rich and stimulating environment where ideas and people could grow and prosper. The United States Department of Labor provided funding for much of the feedback research mentioned in the text. Support for the writing of this book also came from the Faculty Research Fund of the Graduate School of Business, Columbia University.

Last, but most importantly, I thank my wife, Donna, and my daughter, Amy, for their patience, support, and love.

New York, N.Y.   David A. Nadler
June 1977

CONTENTS

**PART 1
INFORMATION AS AN
ORGANIZATIONAL CHANGE TOOL**

1
INFORMATION AND ORGANIZATIONAL CHANGE

Not long ago, the manager of the industrial products division of a manufacturing firm became concerned about what he called "problems of morale" in his organization. Having heard that many organizations use employee surveys as a way of discovering what bothers people, he decided that it might be worthwhile for him to use a questionnaire in his organization. He located a consultant who had previously worked with employee surveys. The manager described the "problems of morale" to the consultant and, after some discussion, the consultant was hired to conduct a survey in the organization.

The consultant decided to use a standardized survey that he had used in many different organizations. He sent copies of the survey and a letter from the division manager to all employees. The employees were to fill out the questionnaire and return it to the consultant. Many employees did not return the questionnaire; however, the consultant felt that a return rate of 50% was good for a mail survey. The consultant had the data from the survey keypunched and run through a computer so that he could analyze the results. He then provided the manager with a large number of descriptive tables and graphs and a short written report which included the consultant's recommendations.

The manager studied the data and the report. All the survey seemed to show was that employees in the lower-level jobs of the organization were dissatisfied; they didn't seem to like their jobs, their

3

supervisors, or their pay. The manager was angry and puzzled. He already knew that these employees were dissatisfied, so that wasn't any news. The survey information presented some interesting points, but he did not know how to use the data. Meanwhile, he heard from members of his staff that since the survey had been administered morale had seemed to drop even lower.

The manager concluded that the survey had not told him anything new. He commented to one of his staff that "Surveys only tell you what you already know. We *know* that there are problems here. What use is there to bringing up those problems over and over again?"

After giving the use of employee surveys some thought, the manager concluded that surveys don't really provide any new insights. In fact, they may even get employees "stirred up" and thinking about problems that they might have been unaware of before. He hoped that any problems caused by the survey would ultimately settle down and decided never to do anything that foolish again.

Unfortunately, this case is not unusual. Many managers have used surveys, questionnaires, or other data-collection devices in the hopes of gathering information that can be used to improve their organizations, only to be frustrated when they fail to learn anything new from the information or are unable to effectively use the information to make changes.

While this particular situation may be discouraging, the experience of many others has provided a very different picture. Information can indeed be a useful tool to help change and improve organizations. However, it is a useful tool only if those in the organization and the consultants that work with them understand why information is important, how data can change behavior, and how to make use of data-based methods for organizational improvement.

As we will see, the division manager's mistake was not in deciding to collect and use data, but in not having a clear idea of *why* he was collecting data, in not having any knowledge of what kind of data to collect, and in not knowing how to use the data once collected. Similarly, the consultant proved to be of little help, because he failed to aid the manager in the critical process of using the information. The basic question is therefore, "How can managers and change agents effectively make use of data for improving organizations?"

This book, which concerns different ways of using information as a tool for organization development (OD), is based on the observation that most effective OD activities involve the elements of data collection, analysis, and feedback on some scale. It is also based on the idea that in order for an organization to change, it must somehow obtain a valid image of itself in the present, develop a clear picture of its problems, and construct realistic maps to guide it toward improvement. This requires data in one form or another; thus data and its uses must be a basic concern for anyone working to help organizations become healthier and more effective.

We will therefore attempt to take a broad view of data and its use in OD, to understand how the use of data brings about changes in behavior, and to examine some of the different approaches or techniques for using data in organizational change. As an introduction, this chapter presents some basic definitions and a set of working assumptions which underlie the rest of the book. There will also be some discussion of the different dimensions of data found in organizations, as well as how data can be used at different stages of an OD relationship.

A STARTING POINT AND SOME DEFINITIONS

Individuals act and organizations function on the basis of information that they receive. People are constantly searching for information to help them make decisions and correct errors, to give them direction, and to confirm their beliefs. In many ways, people are information processors, taking data in and making decisions about behavior. Similarly, organizations are information processing systems. Organizations gather and process environmental data as well as data about internal functioning. Organizational structures perform the function of getting information from one person to another or from one group to another. Information is thus a key factor in the understanding of behavior in organizations.

Given this relationship between information and organizational behavior, it is only natural to think of information's potential value as a tool for the improvement of organizations and for planned organizational change. If information is an important influence on the patterns of behavior of both individuals and organizations, then the use of information may constitute a powerful tool for altering those patterns.

The understanding of how to use data for organizational change can only be considered within the context of a clear definition of some basic concepts. Specifically, there is a need to get a clear idea of what OD is, what we mean when we talk about "process," and what data-based methods are.

Though there are many different definitions of OD (see Bennis, 1969; Beckhard, 1969), it is possible to outline some of its basic characteristics. In general, OD involves a planned and systematic attempt to change patterns of organizational behavior. Its goals are (a) more effective organizational functioning and (b) the improvement of the quality of working life which individuals within the organization experience. OD's basic characteristics include the application of behavioral science knowledge in a collaborative and participative process (usually by a change agent, who frequently is a consultant) in response to some problem or felt need within the organization. Beyond the basic characteristics, the range of possible approaches, activities, and tools is extremely broad.

A change agent usually performs a diagnosis of the client organization. Diagnosis is followed by (or may include) some form of intervention activity, which involves entering into the ongoing behavior of the organization for the purpose of bringing about change. Interventions can be directed at changing individuals, modifying patterns of interaction, affecting informal structures, redesigning formal structures, or changing technical systems. Different interventions can be directed toward the various elements of an organization.

That interaction between people can be analyzed from several different perspectives is a concept closely related to OD. The most obvious perspective is that of *content*—the "what" of the interaction. Another is that of *process*, which is concerned with "how it's happening." As an example, consider a meeting of a group of managers in an organization. A description of the content of the meeting would include the issues discussed, the decisions made, assignments resulting from the meeting, etc. A description of the same meeting in terms of process might involve how frequently different individuals participated, who talked to whom, who performed various leadership functions, how decisions were made, etc.

In general, OD is concerned with process, both process in organizations and the process of intervention. (See Schein, 1969, for an indepth discussion of process and OD.) An underlying notion is that process and content interact, one affecting the other. The concept of process and content is particularly important when using data in OD. As will be seen, how data are collected, who is involved in decisions about the use of data, and how data get fed back all can affect the ultimate usefulness of the information as a change tool.

Data, as used here, will be defined as any form of information which can be collected and is relevant to individual, group, or organizational functioning. Data can take many forms and can be related to different elements, activities, or pursuits of an organization. It is therefore used as a general term to describe the whole range of information available to a manager or change agent.

We will make the case that most OD interventions involve the collection and use of information although it may not be obvious at first. Almost any intervention should include some form of the following activities.

a. *Systematic data collection.* Data may be collected through questionnaires, interviews, observation of behavior, or examination of organizational records. Frequently, these data are an integral part of the change agent's diagnosis of the system, but data may also have other uses.

b. *Data analysis.* The change agent will work with the data, either alone or in collaboration with members of the organization, to aggregate, analyze, or interpret it.

c. *Data feedback.* The change agent will give the data back (perhaps with interpretations) to organization members in a form in which they can make use of it. Data feedback could either be immediate (as when a process consultant gives feedback to a group on its behavior) or delayed (such as computer analysis of questionnaire data or preparation of written reports).

These three steps define what we will call *data-based methods.* Specifically, data-based methods are those activities performed by the change agent which involve *the collection, analysis, and feedback of data in the context of an OD effort.* Although many change agents would not consider themselves to be using data-based methods, gathering, interpreting, and giving back information is indeed characteristic of much OD work. In fact, some change theorists see the generation and use of valid data about organizational functioning as the central, defining characteristic of OD (Argyris, 1970). Different data-based methods are used for different purposes by change agents, and attention must be given to both the content of the information collected and the process of data collection, analysis, and feedback.

Therefore, the focus to be taken here is a broad one as it considers a whole range of data-based methods. Data and data feedback will be considered as tools to be used for bringing about organizational change. As tools, however, data-based methods must be viewed in the context of larger and systematic OD efforts, where the use of data constitutes just one of a number of components.

WORKING ASSUMPTIONS

We will attempt to provide a perspective on the use of data for organizational change. One specific approach or technique will not be advocated. However, the choice of issues, problems, and terms clearly reflects a specific way of looking at organizations and of thinking about change. (See Nadler & Tushman, 1977.) The ideas presented here are based on a view of organizations as open systems. Since that view will shape the discussion and analysis that follows, it is important to express it in a clear and straightforward fashion. One way of doing this is to outline a number of working assumptions that underlie the material throughout the book.

Assumption 1: An Organization is a Complex and Interdependent Open System.   An organization can be viewed as a complex set of interrelated elements called a system. This system consists of social and technical subsystems. It exists and conducts transactions with a larger environment. The concept of a complex open system is abstract, so it may be helpful to consider the following example, which illustrates how an organization is a system. Think for a minute about the industrial products division case discussed at the beginning of this chapter. The organization, as a system, takes certain inputs (such as raw materials) and subjects them to changes (the manufacturing process) to produce outputs (products). The organizational system contains different components or elements (such as people, technology, organizational structure, etc.), and these components or elements are related. For example, people and machines are needed in order for the organization to produce products. The organization includes both social components and subsystems (people, relationships, behavior, structures) and technical components and subsystems (technology, capital, etc.). Finally, in order for the system to function productively it must be involved with other organizations or individuals, such as suppliers, customers, competitors, government regulators, etc.

This means that events or sequences of behavior observed in an organization are the result of multiple causes, both inside and outside the organization. Attempts to change behavior in organizations therefore need to consider these multiple causes and the network of relationships between the different components of an organization. (See Lawrence and Lorsch, 1969, or Galbraith, 1973, for discussions of organization development and organizations as complex systems.)

The systems-theory perspective is important. Because of the interdependence of system components, change is a complex issue. Changing an entire organization does not come about through a single isolated intervention, but through attention to the different but related parts of the system. For example, lasting behavioral changes in the industrial products division would probably not have resulted from attempts to change the people in the division if other elements (such as the production process, the design of jobs, or the compensation system) were ignored.

Systems theory also implies that organizations are capable of adapting and improving over time; as self-correcting mechanisms they have the potential for using information to detect and correct problems. For instance, if the industrial products division were to receive many complaints or fewer orders from its customers, it might possibly make changes in the product design or the production process. Again, an organization is capable of changing in response to information, just as a thermostat changes the operation of a heating unit based on information it gathers about temperature. This view of organizations as self-correcting mechanisms that make use of information is important in understanding why data-based methods work. Information, particularly the collection and use of information, can be useful in helping organizations to change, adapt, and grow.

Assumption 2: Using Data for Organizational Change Involves a Number of Discrete Yet Interdependent Steps.   The use of data for organization development involves a number of separate activities: (1) *choosing the type of data to be collected*; (2) *deciding how to collect the data*; (3) *deciding how to analyze or aggregate the data*; and (4) *determining how the data will be given back to the organization.* Each of these steps is important and will affect ultimate perception, use, and impact of the information on the functioning of the organization. At each step, decisions must be made involving critical questions of both content and process. Thus the sequence should be considered as a whole, since one cannot become involved in one activity without thinking about the others. For example, it would be difficult to discuss what data to collect or what methods of collection to use without some consideration of how the data are to be used, analyzed, or fed back.

Assumption 3: Data-based Methods Form Only One Component of a Systematic Organizational Intervention.   Data-based methods are tools which the change agent uses and which can be applied to a situation for purposes of diagnosis and intervention. Much of the research and a good deal of the experience of change agents seem to indicate that the collection and feedback of data do not of themself lead to lasting organizational change. Systems theory would also indicate that to expect the actions of data collection and feedback to alter a whole set of complex relationships would be unrealistic. The successful use of data-based methods requires that they be used in conjunction with other change tools, ranging from small-group or individual consultation to large system structural change.

Assumption 4: Data-based Methods Need to be Applied Within the Context of the Larger Organizational System.   As with any intervention technique, the use of data-based methods cannot be considered in a vacuum. The decision to collect, analyze, and feed back data is made within the context of a specific organizational setting with existing patterns of decision making, existing structures, existing environments, and existing distributions of power. The issue of power is particularly important since the collection and distribution of data by someone other than the top management of a particular organization present the possibility for a change in the nature of power relationships. Information in many cases is power (Pettigrew, 1972); to make public what few know or to give away privileged information is also to give away power. In our industrial products division example, if the manager were to make the survey data public, he would open up the whole question of what changes should be made. He chose to keep the data private, because releasing it could have reduced his ability to control the situation. Thus using data-based methods is not a simple operation; it involves many political considerations, which in turn have major implications for the success of any OD effort.

Assumption 5: The Process of Using Data-based Methods is Critical.   Who is to have access to what information is frequently a sensitive issue in organizations. Information regarding individual attitudes or perceptions, group performance, or relationships is particularly sensitive. Individuals tend to be concerned (often justifiably) about how such data might be used for or against them. For this reason the process of using data-based methods, or how these methods will be employed, is a critical issue. The manner in which data-based methods are used can affect the perceptions people have of the change agent and his or her activities. It can also affect subsequent reactions to the data. In particular, most people tend to be concerned about the confidentiality of information that is collected from them.

If the data-based methods are used in a way that encourages trust and brings about the frank and honest sharing of information, then the change agent will be in a good position to use the data for diagnosis, planning change, and initiating change. However, if the collection of data is surrounded by mistrust, anxiety, or suspicion, then the data may be of little value for diagnostic, motivational, or planning purposes since people may not trust the data and may react to the information defensively. Data-based interventions are not neutral events in the life of an organization; thus how they are implemented is important.

Assumption 6: Selecting the Appropriate Data-based Methods is Contingent on the Characteristics and Problems of the Particular Client Organization.   There is no one best way of collecting, analyzing, and feeding back data for all situations. As with other OD tools, the intervention must be matched to the diagnosis. In each organizational setting the consultant needs to make an informed choice of what data to collect, how to collect it, how to analyze it, how to feed it back, and whom to feed it back to. In some situations, for example, standardized questionnaires may provide useful data, while in other cases information may only be obtained through direct observation of behavior. When selecting the appropriate data-based method, the following should be considered: (a) the purpose of the data-based process, (b) the specific characteristics of the client's system, and (c) the nature of the immediate problems or felt needs of the client.

THE NATURE OF DATA IN ORGANIZATIONS

So far we have talked about data in very general terms. Looking closer we find that there are many rich sources of data in organizations and many different ways of collecting the various types of information that are available to the change agent. Although our concern will largely be with the process of using data-based methods, it is important to give some attention to the *content* of data collected. Some understanding of the nature of the available data is necessary. There are choices to be made about what kinds of data the change agent should collect when entering a new organizational setting.

Dimension	Characteristics
Subsystem focus	Technical subsystem vs. human subsystem
Point of measurement	Output of system vs. input or transformation processes
Evaluative content	Descriptive vs. evaluative
Aggregation	Individual vs. group vs. total organization
Time orientation	Past vs. present vs. future
Structure of collection	Unstructured collection vs. structured collection
Frequency of collection	One time vs. continuous
Sampling of variables	Narrow sampling vs. broad sampling
Validity	Valid vs. invalid
Access	Limited vs. unlimited

Fig. 1.1   Types of data in organizations.

There are various ways of categorizing data. A complete list of the different kinds of data in organizations would be lengthy. The basic question is "How does information differ?"; that is, "What are its various characteristics?" Figure 1.1 lists some of the potential characteristics of data found in organizations. Descriptions of the various types of information follow.

Subsystem Focus: Which part of the organizational system is to be the focal point for obtaining the information? One specific type of data concerns the functioning of the technical system and includes budget information, performance measures, reject rates, raw material costs, work-flow measures, etc. Another type of data reflects the functioning of the social system and includes data on the organizational structure, as well as on individual feelings, attitudes and behavior, group functioning, etc.

Point of Measurement: Whether looking at the technical or social system within the organization, is the data focused on the output of the system (the final product) or on the input or transformation process of the system? Output data could include information about the number of products produced, earnings, employee satisfaction, etc. Input or transformation process data could include information about production costs, work flow, group dynamics, leadership practices, quality of raw material, etc.

Evaluative Content: What is the difference in the degree to which various pieces of information describe behavior in relatively objective terms? Does the information focus on description or on interpretation and evaluation? Descriptive data can usually be verified by obtaining convergent information which describes the same events. If the data are evaluative, then it becomes important to understand the behavior, position, and motivation of the source of the information before interpreting it.

Aggregation: How can the information concerning organizational functioning be aggregated? One can observe the behavior of individuals or groups, the behavior that exists between groups, and the behavior or functioning of the total organizational system in a larger environment. Data can be aggregated at different levels and thus may reflect the functioning of an organization at any of these different levels. When analyzing the data, it can be aggregated in different ways to provide information about certain groups or functions.

Time Orientation: Does the information vary in its time orientation? Events which occurred in the past, current states or activities, or information about the future may be reported.

Structure of Collection: Does the structure of the method of collection vary? Data of predetermined scope or nature can be collected in a formally structured manner and summarized in quantitative terms. For example, accounting measures or close-ended employee questionnaires are structured forms. Data can also be collected in much less structured ways. This type of information is less predictable in form, inconsistent in occurrence, and often less amenable to quantitative manipulation. Included in this category might be a change agent's impression of an organization, the process consultant's observations of group functioning, or the examination of written communications. Thus the degree to which data are structured or the degree of amenability to structured collection varies.

Frequency of Collection: At what time intervals are data collected? The "one-shot" collection of data at a single point in time, such as during a single set of interviews, is one extreme of the frequency of collection. At the other extreme is the continuous collection of data. Two examples of continuous collection of data would be (1) the monitoring of absenteeism records and (2) a participant observer who keeps a daily journal.

Sampling of Variables: What issues are covered by the data that are collected? There are logistical limits as to how much data can be collected and analyzed by one change agent or group of change agents. Thus, as the data collector makes choices within certain dimensions, a sampling plan begins to evolve. This is not a sampling of people, rather it concerns the sampling of issues or what might be called variables. Some variables will be sampled; others will not. The questions are how broadly to sample and how to decide which variables to include and which to exclude. A basic question here is, "Does the change agent have an underlying model of organizations to guide him or her in the sampling and to ensure that critical variables are not omitted?''

Validity: Is the information seen as accurate, consistent, and undistorted? The issue of the validity of information is a complex one. How much "objective" validity does the information have (tested by scientific or statistical procedures)? How much "perceived" validity does the information have (tested by verifying with organization members whether the data are seen as accurate)? Both types of validation are important.

Access: Who is to have access to the information? Once the information is collected, is it to be accessible to everyone in the organization or only to a very limited few? The degree of accessibility which organization members have to the data may affect its perceived validity and ultimate use.

Any data which a consultant collects can therefore be classified within these dimensions. The range of data available in organizations is broad, and the options are many. The change agent makes a choice (whether conscious or not) every time he or she decides to collect or study data. This choice is a double-edged one, since every affirmative choice to collect a certain type of data in a certain manner also involves an implicit choice to ignore other types of data or to not use other methods of collection.

It is not possible to say what kinds of data change agents should collect in all situations; there are, however, several factors which should be considered. First, the change agent should have some kind of underlying model of both organizations and change. Having a model guides one in the choice of variables and in the choice of data-collection methods. Second, the choice of what data to collect needs to be guided by ongoing diagnostic judgments of the change agent. By sensing and continually testing the nature of the client's problems, the change agent will be guided to useful data. Third, organizational members (both managers and employees) are excellent sources of guidance. They frequently have a very good "feel" for the type of information that would be useful and how to obtain it. Finally, the choice of the type of information to be collected and how to collect it should be made based on how far the consulting relationship has progressed. For example, during the early diagnostic work, different kinds of data may be more useful than later on during an evaluative phase. (Chapter 5 gives a detailed discussion of how decisions concerning data collection are made.)

The range of data available to the change agent serves to underscore the importance of not over-relying on one specific source of information or type of data, whether it is a structured questionnaire or a consultant's clinical judgments. Any one type of information cannot be fully descriptive of the functioning of a complex organizational system.

THE USES OF DATA IN THE CHANGE PROCESS

The various kinds of data that are available to the change agent can be used in many different ways to facilitate organizational change. Different types of data are used at different stages of the OD process. Different models describe the sequence of events that occur in the typical OD program. One useful model, developed by Kolb and Frohman (1970), describes seven steps in an OD/consulting relationship:

1) scouting,

2) entry,

3) diagnosis,

4) planning,

5) action,

6) evaluation, and

7) termination.

Obviously, real-life events do not always fall into a neat and orderly sequence. As pointed out by Schein (1969), initial interactions relating to entry also provide diagnostic data, as well as opportunities to start interventions. A model, however, allows us to visualize the different kinds of activities that frequently occur.

Figure 1.2 indicates some of the major uses and types of data which correspond to different OD stages. Some major uses of data and examples from actual experiences follow.

Stages of OD (from Kolb & Frohman, 1970)	Typical use of data
Scouting/Entry	*Orientation:* data used to get a feel for the client organization's basic characteristics and to find out if there is a basis for a relationship.
Diagnosis	*Diagnosis:* data used to develop a comprehensive and in-depth picture of the client's system: its operations, its employee's attitudes, its strong points, and its major problems and their causes.
Planning	*Planning interventions:* data used to determine what interventions are appropriate, where they should be applied, and how they should be implemented.
Action	*Motivating change:* data used to motivate individuals or groups to unfreeze or begin changing and to initiate the change process.
Evaluation/Termination	*Monitoring and assessing interventions:* data used to track the progress of interventions as they are implemented and to assess the costs and benefits of interventions after they are completed.

Fig. 1.2   Uses of data in different stages of OD.

Orientation: One of the first things a change agent must do when beginning work with a new client is to get a feel for the nature of the client's system. In a sense the change agent is trying to determine the "lay of the land." This is an important activity. By obtaining information about the client organization, sensing what some of its needs are, and understanding the viewpoints of members of the system, the change agent can begin to determine what the nature of the contract with the client will be, what resources will be needed, and whether his or her expertise will be responsive to the needs of the client. Data about the system can be collected by observation, from initial interactions with the client (Alderfer, 1968), and from discussions with various members of the organization. During the orientation stage sampling of variables will typically be very broad, and the methods of collection will be unstructured. The change agent may also have to work with evaluative information of perceived and objective validity.

An example of the use of data for orientation purposes can be seen in the recent experience of two change agents who were asked by the director of a voluntary community service agency to help him with "organizational problems." In order to get a feel for what those organizational problems were and whether there was a basis for a consulting relationship, the two consultants began by visiting the agency several times. They observed staff meetings, talked to paid and volunteer staff and community members, and observed the director as he performed some of his duties. Only after this initial, informal data-collection activity were the consultants able to determine that their skills might be helpful and to develop a written proposal for working with the client. Because of this initial data, the consultants were also able to specify which groups had to give their consent before the project could start.

Diagnosis: An important step in any OD activity is conducting an in-depth and comprehensive diagnosis of the client organization. The process of diagnosis is essentially one of data collection, analysis, and validation. The results of the diagnosis are then used by the change agent and client to determine what general kinds of interventions might be appropriate. The major activity of diagnosis is the collection of data about how the system operates—what seems to be going well, what seem to be causes of the problems, and what are the perceptions and feelings of people in the system? In this stage sampling is still fairly broad, but it is necessary to have a diagnostic model for guidance in the selection of variables. It is important to obtain descriptive data of high validity. A variety of structured and unstructured collection methods can be used.

There are many examples of data collection for diagnosis and various frameworks exist for collecting diagnostic data. One example can be seen in the activities of a university-based group of consultants, who worked with a community mental-health center to discover what kinds of problems existed in the organization. Using a comprehensive diagnostic model (Levinson, 1972), the group spent eight months observing behavior, conducting interviews, sitting in on meetings, going over organizational records, and administering questionnaires. After integrating the information, the group was able to present an in-depth picture of the center as a social and technical system and was also able to identify the key areas of the system where problems seemed to exist.

Planning Interventions: The planning of specific intervention activities is another important step in organization development. Data collected from diagnostic activities as well as that collected for the specific purpose of planning intervention activities can be used to identify the specific nature of problems, to discover appropriate steps of action, and to help in deciding how the steps can be implemented. In planning intervention activities, a very narrow range of variables is sampled. Validity remains a very important factor. Participative planning for change also requires accessible information.

> For example, in the area of job enrichment, the initial diagnostic process may indicate that some of the employees seem to be dissatisfied with the type of work they perform or that a lack of motivation seems to be associated with certain groups who perform certain types of jobs. Before the redesign work can begin, it must be determined which jobs need to be redesigned, which jobs are amenable to redesign, who desires the redesigned jobs, and what specific dimensions of the jobs are in need of redesign. Again, standardized collection methods for this information exist (Hackman and Oldham, 1975), and data collected in this way can serve as tools for planning specific work redesign interventions.

Motivating Change: Change is most likely to occur in an organization when individuals feel a need to change or are motivated to collaborate in diagnostic or intervention activities. This "unfreezing" is essential to the change process. Information plays an important role in unfreezing or motivating change. (Bennis, Berlew, Schein, and Steele, 1973); specifically, information which is seen as valid, accurate, and unbiased and which presents a new and different picture of an organization can be a powerful and motivating force in bringing about change. Thus information that is perceived as valid can be used to make individuals aware of problems and the possibilities for change. This particular use of data is relevant to the action stage of change; however, data can be used at any point in the process (from scouting and entry to termination) to motivate change.

As part of a larger project, a group of consultant/researchers initiated a combination performance and survey feedback system in a number of bank branch offices. A dramatic example of the "unfreezing" effects of information was seen when one branch received its first feedback report. It indicated that of the ten branches its performance and level of employee perception and attitude were the lowest. After receiving this report, management and employees suddenly began extensive activity, including group meetings, problem-solving sessions, etc., to try to identify problems and work collaboratively on solutions to improve the functioning of the branch and to make it a better place to work. The new, valid (though negative) information was a powerful motivator for both managers and employees.

Monitoring the Progress of Interventions: Data can be used to monitor or trace the progress of interventions as they unfold over time. Data, collected by various methods, can be used to determine how the intervention activities are being perceived, whether the intervention is being taken seriously, what effects are occurring in terms of attitudes and performance, and what kinds of problems are being experienced. This information, narrowly sampled and taken at frequent intervals, can be used to modify or make mid-course corrections in an intervention.

A systematic attempt at using data for monitoring interventions was performed in a pharmaceutical plant where a consultant was assisting in the implementation of a "participative-management" system. As the monitoring was done in the various departments of the plant, a short one-page survey was distributed to department members on a monthly basis. The results of the survey and observations (for more than a year) of behavior in the plant enabled conclusions to be drawn concerning the effect different activities had on the organization.

Assessing the Effects of Interventions: Data can be used for purposes of evaluation. Systematically collected information can be used to determine what the effects of OD interventions have been, to determine the costs and benefits of the change and to learn from both the successes and failures. Again, a broad sampling and scientific validity of the data are required.

> A large public utility (in conjunction with a consulting firm) became involved in organizational-design work. Under the guidance of a joint labor-management committee, the consulting team worked with organization members to examine the work flow, identify problem areas, reorganize the department structure, and create an organization design more appropriate to the nature of the work being done and more responsive to the demands of the environment. Data were used to evaluate the effects of the structural changes, including an analysis of the work flow before and after the changes, an analysis of project costs and completion times before and after the changes, and an examination of employee attitudes and perceptions accomplished with the use of questionnaires and interviews before and after the reorganization.

Thus information has different uses in different stages of OD work. As seen above, information can be used to orient the change agent, diagnose organizational problems, plan interventions, initiate or motivate change, monitor the course of interventions, and evaluate the effects of interventions. Data therefore serve as tools for the change agent, to be used along with other intervention tools, approaches, or techniques. Information can also be used as a guide to determine where and when to apply other intervention technologies.

SUMMARY

The argument presented here is that information is an important factor in organizational life and that the use of information for planned organizational change is therefore an area worth thinking about. A set of explicit working assumptions, which present one way of thinking about data and organizational change, has been given. Underlying these assumptions is the image of an organization as a complex open system where only comprehensive multifaceted interventions can bring about lasting and durable change. Within this framework, data-based methods are seen as one tool which should be considered within the context of the particular organizational system and which should be used as appropriate for the specific characteristics and needs of the client.

2
CASE EXAMPLES OF DATA-BASED METHODS

How are data-based methods actually used in organizations? Thus far, our major concern has been "making a case" for the importance of data in organization development. We have discussed why data are important, what kinds of data exist in organizations, and how data can be used at different stages of an organization development relationship. The central purpose of this book, however, is not to justify or argue for the use of data-based methods; its goal is to help people learn how to use these methods effectively. Three questions become particularly important at this point:

1. *"What is it?"* What are data-based methods? What characteristics do different approaches to using data have in common?

2. *"Why does it work?"* Why should the use of information lead to changes in the patterns of behavior in organizations?

3. *"How can it be used effectively?"* This is perhaps the most important question. Based on an understanding of what data-based methods are and why they have the potential to change behavior, how can these methods best be used to identify and solve organizational problems?

Three brief case studies of actual interventions, where the central theme of each is the use of data-based methods, are presented as a first step in answering the question, "What is it?" These case studies illustrate the different degrees of success that can be achieved. They will also illustrate a range of situations, data, organizations, and approaches. They should provide an understanding of what data-based change is and how data-based methods are used. These case studies will be used as references throughout the later discussions of why and how data can be used for change.

WINFIELD SCHOOL DISTRICT*

The Winfield School District is one of three districts in a large school system. The district superintendent reports to the chief school officer, who is the head of the entire school system. The district consists of 18 schools, ranging in size from relatively small elementary schools to a high school with 62 faculty members and 1100 students.

Interest in organization development grew after a member of the district superintendent's staff attended a summer workshop designed to give school administrators an overview of how behavioral science techniques could be used to increase both teacher productivity and job satisfaction. Following the workshop, the district superintendent contacted the consultant* who had conducted the program and discussed the possibility of launching an OD project in the Winfield School District. After considerable discussion, they agreed to have the consultant design a formal proposal, which would outline the major stages of activity. The project would involve the entire school district and would include the use of an employee-attitude questionnaire to identify problem areas and facilitate problem solving throughout the district. The consultant's proposal outlined a structured plan to be used by the district personnel.

Following are some proposal excerpts which provide insight into the specific elements of the project and the model the consultant planned to use.

_____

*   Names in this case have been changed to protect the confidentiality of those concerned. Information was provided by Jay N. Nisberg, who served as the external consultant in the case.

PROPOSAL TO WINFIELD SCHOOL DISTRICT

A. *Objective:*   The objective of the organization development effort is to help administrators, teachers, and other personnel improve the organizational and professional functioning of the school by using a survey feedback program.

B. *Program Description:*   The survey feedback program is designed to help an organization systematically identify its process and product needs and to develop action plans to meet these needs. The program maximizes involvement of all members of the organization. The system assumes responsibility for managing and giving direction to the program. Built into the model is a component to help the system build the organizational competence needed to carry out the developmental process. The program is composed of two major components: program delivery and facilitator training.

1. *Program delivery:*   The major steps of the process are represented in Fig. 2.1.

   a. Orientation: Acquaint personnel with the program and deal with questions and concerns.

   b. Survey data collection: Conduct an attitude survey.

   c. Data measure: Prepare data for feedback to teachers and administrators and determine success measurements.

   d. Work group leader preparation: Train leaders to deal with data, feedback methods, and action planning.

   e. Feedback: Feed data back to individual work groups.

   f. Evaluation: Evaluate the selected criteria for success.

   g. Work group action planning: Planning by individual work groups based on data collected.

   h. Resurvey data collection: Conduct second attitude survey to determine changes and initiate future action planning.

   i. Diffusion: Continue self-renewing organizational process.

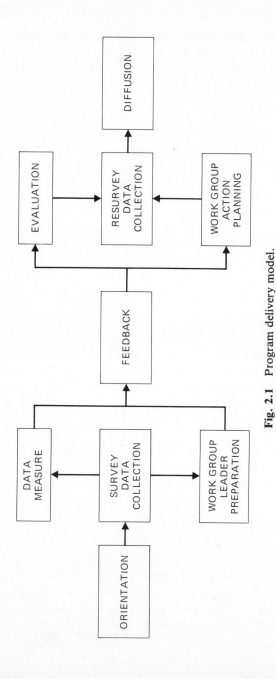

Fig. 2.1   Program delivery model.

2. *Facilitator training:* This is an intensive training program for approximately 20 people from the Winfield School District to facilitate the organization development program described above. The training would consist of a series of workshops and consultations to give program-delivery facilitators the conceptual and operational skills necessary to facilitate the process within the system.

The proposal also called for voluntary participation by staff members of individual schools in a district steering committee (composed of teachers and administrators) to oversee the entire project and in school steering committees to direct the project within individual schools.

The proposal was reviewed by district staff members and discussions were begun with other relevant groups. The teachers' advisory council (a group of teachers from different schools who provided teacher input at the district level) was consulted and the project was approved.

During these discussions, more detailed work was done on the feedback model. It was decided that preliminary planning for what type of data to collect and how to make use of data would be conducted on a school-by-school basis by the school steering committee, a task which would involve many of the staff members in planning for the survey work. Data were to be collected from organizational members on a voluntary and confidential basis. Data would first be fed back to top-level personnel and then down through the hierarchy in functional teams or work groups at "action planning meetings." Each work group leader would hold a meeting with his or her colleagues during which the survey data would be discussed. Several things were to happen at the meetings: (a) participants would be asked to interpret the data; (b) plans would be made for implementing constructive changes; and, (c) plans would be made for data feedback to the next level down. During these meetings a consultant or resource person (usually a member of a school steering committee) would be present if invited into the meeting by the participants.

Finally, the district superintendent and the external consultant jointly defined "success criteria." These were factors that would be used to evaluate the effectiveness of the feedback process and included the following:

a. Changes in perceptions of team functioning by work group members.

b. Decreases in teacher absenteeism.

c. Changes in data from survey 1 to survey 2.

d. Changes in the schools' departmental structures.

e. Diffusion of the survey feedback process throughout Winfield School District.

f. Degree to which action plans were actually implemented.

By early September, the decision was made to go ahead with the OD program and a contract (a modification of the earlier proposal) was agreed upon. The project was ready to begin. All interested staff members were invited to an orientation meeting which was held to describe the project elements, and representatives from six schools attended. The program was reviewed, the model was described, and facilitator-training was discussed. The program delivery model called for the school steering committee members to attend the facilitator training program. The program paralleled the nine steps in the model (orientation, survey data collection, etc.) with approximately one day devoted to each step of the model. The training days were spread out over the school year so that the facilitators could attend a day of training and return to their school to implement the next step of the process; then go back for training on the next step in the model and return to their school to implement it, etc.

According to the external consultant this meeting, as well as the lengthy discussions concerning the contract, were important since he felt that there would be a strong relationship between the level of understanding about the project and project success.

Following this meeting, the individual schools began their projects, each having variations determined by the needs of the school. For example, in the early fall, the high school formed a steering committee which included two department heads, two administrators, one staff person, and three teachers. This group met in October and November to clarify project elements, to ascertain their understanding of the basic concepts, and to make critical decisions as to how the project should proceed in their school. In November the steering committee held a meeting for the entire staff, where they explained the project and the procedures to be used, and answered questions. In December the steering committee reviewed a number of different standardized questionnaires provided by the consultant and then proceeded to design their own survey of about 120 items. This survey was reviewed by the consultant and reproduced and administered to the staff in January. Also during January, the steering committee conducted workshops for the work group leaders who would have to facilitate the groups that would work with the data. In February the data were returned to the participants and work group meetings began.

The work group meetings seemed to be successful. First each group worked on interpreting and combining the data with their feelings and perceptions to identify critical problems in the organization. Groups then began to generate possible changes that might help solve the problems. Where changes involved areas under the control of the work group (for example, selection of textbooks, curriculum design, etc.), the groups were free to implement their own changes. Where changes involved the entire school, proposals in the form of "action plans" were submitted to the school principal.

By June, when the survey was readministered, a number of action plans had been developed and some had been implemented. School personnel were beginning to feel that the organization was definitely improving and becoming more effective.

NORTHEASTERN HOSPITAL*

Northeastern Hospital is a moderate-sized institution located on the outskirts of a major city. It is a specialized chronic disease and rehabilitation hospital which only admits patients who fall into one of these two categories. Patients with chronic diseases account for about two-thirds of the total number admitted and require long-term care, especially nursing care. Many of these patients have terminal illnesses. Patients requiring rehabilitation are mainly individuals who have suffered from accidents or injuries; following immediate emergency treatment or surgery they are admitted to Northeastern to undergo an intensive program of rehabilitation, guided by physicians, physical therapists, and occupational therapists. The hospital has approxi-

---

*   Names in this case have been changed to protect confidentiality of those involved.

mately 300 beds and a total staff of about 600. Northeastern Hospital is affiliated with a religious organization, which is a major source of its financial support.

A few years ago, the top management of Northeastern became concerned about a number of organizational and personnel problems within the hospital. The hospital administrator, Dennis Rettew, was concerned about high levels of employee turnover and absenteeism, an inability to recruit personnel for the nursing staff, poor communications, low levels of morale, and increasing talk of union activity. Rettew was particularly concerned about problems in the nursing service.

During one summer, Rettew began discussions with a consultant affiliated with a nearby university about some of the problems as he saw them. Together they explored the possibility of a consulting relationship. Finally they agreed that the consultant should put together a team of three individuals, also affiliated with the university, to serve as a consulting group for the hospital. This group, which soon became known as the "university team," was to conduct an intensive diagnostic study of the hospital as an organization. This diagnostic work would serve as the basis for additional activities to improve the functioning of the hospital.

In September the university team met with the hospital's executive committee, a group made up of individuals who reported directly to the administrator, including the medical director, the director of nursing, the manager of finance, etc. The university team described their goal of helping the hospital obtain an accurate picture of itself as a human organization so that improvements could be made. The consultants discussed their strategy for diagnosis and feedback of the data.

In the first stage they proposed holding orientation meetings with each hospital work group. One or two members of the team would meet with a work group (for example, a nursing shift on a ward) to introduce themselves, describe the goals of the project, describe the data-collection activities that would occur, and answer any questions that individuals might have.

The second stage would involve data collection. It was proposed that a sample of employees be interviewed in depth, that all employees be given a short questionnaire, that the team have access to hospital records, and that team members be allowed to observe people at work, both on the job and at meetings.

The third stage involved feedback. The consultant team discussed its intention to prepare a written report based on an analysis of the data collected. They also proposed that all employees who participated receive feedback about the results of the study. After some discussion, the executive committee approved the plan. Although some members stated that "this type of study won't tell us anything we don't already know," most agreed that such a project could do little harm and might even be helpful.

In October, the university team began its work. Each team member spent about 15 hours a week at the hospital. As a first step, orientation meetings were held with all work groups. The team members stressed to employees that all data collected would be kept confidential, but that a written report describing the results and making recommendations would be produced after the data had been collected and analyzed. Employees responded well to the team, and many actually seemed anxious to tell team members about problems they had been encountering.

By November, the interviews were started. Rettew had provided the team with an office in the hospital from which to work, and the team began conducting two-hour interviews with a randomly sampled group of employees, representing all levels and departments of the hospital. Approximately 100 people were interviewed. After each interview, the team member who interviewed each employee visited the employee at his or her job location and spent two hours observing the person at work.

In December a standardized questionnaire, which included 30 statements about working in the hospital, was administered. For each statement the employee was to mark one of five possible responses indicating how often the activity described in the statement *actually* occurred. For example, one statement was "supervisors listen to people as well as direct them." For this statement, each employee was to indicate whether this happened *always, frequently, occasionally, seldom,* or *never.* The employee also marked another set of responses for the same statement, this time indicating how often this activity *should* occur.

Data collection continued through January and February, concentrating on direct observation of behavior and analysis of hospital records. Employees were observed at work and at important group meetings. The director of the university team also met weekly with

Rettew to report on progress and to obtain help in scheduling additional data-collection activities.

As the team began to put the data together, they identified a number of major problems in the organization. One set of problems was related to top management and the functioning of the executive committee. Members of the executive committee seemed to be confused about their roles and the degree of decision-making authority they had. Many shared the perception that all of the important decisions were made (prior to meetings) by Rettew. Many also perceived that major decisions were made behind closed doors, and that Rettew often made "side deals" with different individuals, promising them special favors or rewards in return for support at the committee meetings. People at this level felt manipulated, confused, and dissatisfied.

Major problems also existed in the nursing service. The director of nursing seemed to be patterning her managerial style after that of Rettew. The nursing staff felt particularly dissatisfied. Nursing supervisors and head nurses felt that they had no authority, while staff nurses complained about a lack of direction and openness by the nursing administration. The structure of the organization was unclear. Nurses were unsure of what their jobs were, whom they should report to, and how decisions were made.

Based on these and other findings, the team put together a 26-page feedback report containing 11 tables and charts which illustrated some of the findings. This report described how the data were collected, and the major patterns observed in the data. It also presented conclusions and recommendations for changes in the hospital. The team chose not to directly address the issue of Rettew's managerial style in the written report, but did make suggestions for changes in the way decisions were made as well as suggestions for the clarification of top managers' roles. The report did, however, include a detailed discussion of problems in the nursing area.

Copies of the report were submitted to Rettew and the executive committee. The team spent several hours working with the group, discussing the findings and the implications of the report and the recommendations made. During these meetings, some committee members reacted positively to the report, while others, such as the director of nursing, became more and more anxious as the discussions continued. During one of the last meetings, the director of nursing walked into the meeting with a thick book on hospital administration under her arm and began attacking the consultant team, claiming that all of their knowledge about organizations was not really applicable to hospitals, because hospitals are different from other kinds of organizations.

A final issue to be discussed with the executive committee was that of feedback. The consultants assumed that copies of their report would be made available to all members of the organization. However, members of the executive committee felt differently. They perceived that the original agreement to give everyone feedback never was intended to guarantee *written* feedback to everyone. Several of the committee members felt that the report could be a "bombshell" and that to make the findings of the report public would create unrest and actually provide ammunition for those employees in nursing who were agitating for a union. Despite the protests of the consultants, the committee refused to allow copies of the report to be distributed to anyone outside of the executive committee. Meetings would be held at which the report could be read aloud, but no copies of the report or the attached charts and tables would be distributed.

In the meantime, the hospital employees were showing an increased interest in the project and were beginning to discuss the long-awaited consultants' report. They awaited the feedback with great anticipation, hoping that the study would bring to the surface many important problems that could then be solved.

In April, a series of feedback meetings were held in the hospital. The executive committee insisted on scheduling the meetings because of the implications of having large numbers of employees away from their jobs at one time. Six different meetings, each including 60 to 100 people from different work units, were held. The consultants read the report to each group, presenting charts and graphs using overhead projections; they then entertained questions and discussion from each group. Members of the executive committee were present (at the rear of the room) for all meetings.

During the first few meetings there was a great deal of discussion, and many questions were asked about why the report was not distributed and what would happen after the meetings. The executive committee members responded, saying that the executive committee would consider the report and its recommendations and would take appropriate action. As the meetings progressed, participation decreased. A rumor developed that people who spoke up at the meetings would "pay for it" later, once the consultants had left. The final meetings were characterized by a lack of employee participation—few questions and little discussion—and discouragement on the part of employees.

The executive committee, in its final meeting with the consultants, thanked them for doing a thorough job and assured them that their recommendations would be seriously considered.

Six months later one of the consultants encountered a group of nurses from Northeastern Hospital on their day off. Upon inquiring about the project, the consultant found that nothing concrete had happened after the university team left and that a number of the more vocal nurses in the service had since left the hospital for other jobs.

PEOPLE'S NATIONAL BANK*

People's National Bank (PNB) is a large bank in a moderate-sized midwestern city. PNB was approached by a group of consultant/researchers from a nearby university who were interested in trying some new approaches to organization development based on the construction of ongoing feedback systems in organizations to aid in group problem solving. The PNB staff wanted to improve the functioning of their retail branch banking system (composed of 20 branches), and they expressed interest in a project of this sort. Meetings were held during which the researchers presented their ideas to a number of top-level bank executives.

It was decided during these initial discussions that the objectives of the project would be:

1. to develop a feedback system that would increase the availability of information to employees and management;

2. to develop a feedback system that would include information about the human organization and employee behavior as well as the more traditional financial information;

---

*   Names in this case have been changed to protect the confidentiality of those involved. Excerpted by permission of the publisher from "The ongoing feedback system: Experimenting with a new managerial tool" by David A. Nadler, Philip H. Mirvis, and Cortlandt Cammann. *Organization Dynamics,* Spring 1976, © 1976 by AMACOM, a division of American Management Associations.

3. to develop a feedback system that conveyed only useful information to the recipients.

It further was decided to introduce the feedback system experimentally in the bank's branch system in order to study its effects. Ten bank branches would receive the feedback and ten would serve as controls. After about a year of operation, the research team would conduct an extensive evaluation to determine the effects of the system.

Finally, it was decided that the system would be designed by a task force composed of eight employees (two tellers, one loan interviewer, two teller supervisors, one assistant branch manager, and two branch managers) selected from different branches, the management coordinator for the project (who reported to the vice president for branch operations), and the three researchers. This task force was to review existing measurements, design new measures where necessary, and develop a feedback system based on the approach previously developed by the researchers.

The members were chosen for the task force, and the research team made a presentation in which they described the experiment at each of the experimental and control branches. Employees were asked to complete a questionnaire that would be used as a baseline measure in evaluating the effects of the experiment.

The Design Phase

The design phase began in February with an intensive series of meetings during which the task force developed a clear-cut set of goals, a timetable for completion, and a contract describing how the group would work. These early meetings were crucial to the success of the task force because groups of this type were unique within the bank and the status differences between group members constituted a significant barrier to full participation. The task-force members, including the research team members, found these initial meetings uncomfortable and frustrating, but they resulted in clearly defined goals for the task force and a high level of participation by all team members.

After the initial meetings, the task force met for two hours each week. Over a two-month period, the task force designed the basic elements of the feedback system. It made decisions about the information to be included in the system, how the information should be distributed, and the types of comparative information that should be fed back along with branch performance data.

An interesting aspect of this process was the considerable discussion and frequent disagreement at the meetings about the measures to be included in the system. At times, the task-force members of lower status (tellers) were able to openly disagree with higher-status members (branch managers) and were thus able to influence the measures ultimately incorporated in the feedback system. For example, it was debated whether to include information on employees' intentions of leaving their jobs in the feedback report. Lower-level employees felt that this information would encourage management to be sensitive to employee problems. Management members, however, felt that publicizing the figures on potential turnover might encourage grievances, unionization, and employee dissatisfaction; they therefore opposed the inclusion of such a question in the feedback questionnaire. Three weeks were spent discussing this issue and, in the end, the lower-level employees on the task force convinced management of the measure's usefulness.

As a result of the task force's effort and the open climate in the group, the set of feedback measures adopted seemed to reflect the input of all task force members and formed the core of an innovative, ongoing feedback system (see Fig. 2.2).

The feedback measures covered four different areas:

1. Performance information reflecting branch performance in the loan area (that is, loan volume, delinquency rates, and so on).

2. Performance information reflecting branch performance in the teller area (balancing records, number of transactions, and so on).

3. Performance information reflecting overall branch performance in terms of employee behavior (rates of absenteeism and turnover), employee effectiveness (quality of customer service), and branch performance in financial terms (overall branch profitability).

4. Attitudinal information based on questionnaire data that reflected the organizational process in the branches (adequacy of communication within the various branches).

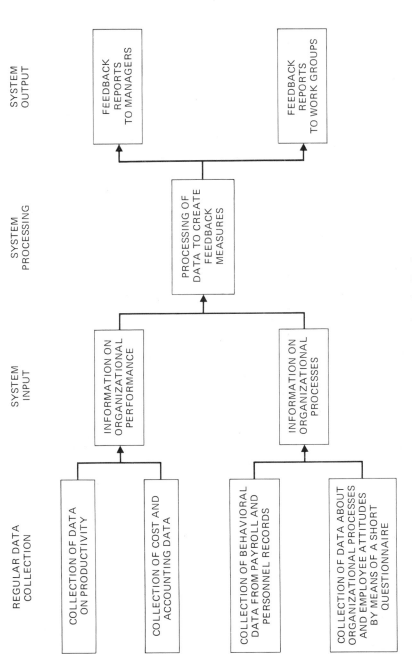

Fig. 2.2 Model of an ongoing feedback system.

Each of these areas was covered in a four-page computer-output feedback report.

In addition to deciding which information would be included in the system, the task force determined:

1. Feedback would be provided monthly, since monthly feedback was standard procedure for the financial systems in the bank.

2. The focus would be on problem solving, not on performance evaluation, and thus the feedback would cover branch rather than individual performance.

3. The feedback measures, wherever feasible, would be accompanied by comparisons to aid in interpreting the information. Appropriate comparisons were developed for most of the measures, often focusing on the past performance of the branch itself to highlight trends.

4. The feedback would be made available in some form to all employees in the experimental branches.

5. Each month, each employee in an experimental branch would fill out a short questionnaire describing the branch climate and leadership, and his or her own attitudes. This questionnaire which required anonymous participation would be the basis for feedback of attitudinal data.

Implementation Phase

The implementation phase involved three steps.

1. *The Actual Procedures Necessary for Collecting and Processing the Feedback Information Were Developed and Tested.* By early May, the bank's computer group had designed the procedures and May-feedback reports were prepared on a trial basis. The feedback system began operating in June, and in mid-July the June-feedback reports were returned to the branches.

2. *Personnel in the Experimental Branches Were Familiarized With the Feedback System.* In late May and early June, the task force members held meetings in each of the experimental branches during which they outlined the purpose of the feedback system, the way the

system had evolved, and what would be expected of the branch members each month. This was done to ensure that branch employees would understand the feedback system before they began working with it.

3. *The Branch Managers, Assistant Managers, and Teller Supervisors Were Trained to Use the System.* Each member of management in the experimental branches and the task-force members attended one of two 5-hour training sessions conducted by the research team. During these sessions, system measures were explained in detail. There was also extensive discussion on the ways in which the feedback information could be used in the branches. The discussion focused on the following points: (1) the importance of actively using the feedback system; (2) the importance of using information from the past as a basis for solving future problems rather than as a basis for evaluating past performance; (3) techniques for running feedback sessions so that they would involve all employees and facilitate problem solving; (4) ways in which the feedback to the branches—including charts to illustrate trends in performance, types of meetings to be held, ways in which responsibility for running the system could be delegated, and so on—should be handled.

Step 3 in the implementation process is an important one. The responsibility for using the feedback system in the branches would rest primarily with the managers and supervisors. The purpose of the training session was to make them aware of the available options and potential pitfalls.

The feedback system was completely installed by June. The research team, aside from infrequent visits to interview managers on their experiences with the new system, was not involved in the actual activities at the branches.

A year later, the research team collected some additional data and began to evaluate the effects of the system. They found that not all of the branches had actively or effectively used the system. Five of the branches had used the system a great deal. Meetings were held regularly to work with the data, and both managers and employees felt that major improvements had been made in the operation of those branches. In the other five branches, the system was either not used or used only halfheartedly; employees saw little improvement or change.

The questionnaire and performance data showed that, in the teller-operations area, improvements in efficiency, turnover, and attitudes came only in those branches where the system was actively used. In the lending activities of the branches, however, increases in productivity (loan volume), relative to the control branches (those not having the feedback system), occurred in almost all of the branches receiving feedback. Both the research team and bank personnel concluded that a feedback system could be a useful tool for organizational change and improvement, but it could only be fully effective if managers had the skills and motivation needed to use the data effectively.

3
THE DATA-COLLECTION/FEEDBACK CYCLE

There are many ways of using data for organization development. In the three cases just examined, different types of data were used, ranging from questionnaire data at the Winfield School District to selected performance and attitude measures at PNB, to comprehensive social and technical information at Northeastern Hospital. Similarly, different approaches for working with the data were used.

The consultants at Northeastern Hospital took the responsibility for the feedback of information to employees, but were constrained by management's concern and the lack of a clear mandate in the hospital. The consultant working with the Winfield School District worked with people in the organization to structure a process for using data, largely by relying on small groups. The team in PNB purposely left issues of data usage up to each branch manager, providing only general guidance through a training program. As we will see, some of these differences (in the type of data collected and how data were used) were critical to the success or failure of the interventions.

While the examination of differences in collecting and using data is useful, it is important to begin with some agreement on what characteristics define the use of data-based methods. In other words, it is important to see how various ways of using data are similar before looking at how they differ.

In this chapter, some of the basic similarities which cut across different ways of using data will be examined. First, a model of the steps involved in collecting, analyzing, and using data will be presented. This model should provide a basic framework for understanding what kinds of choices consultants and organizations face when they use data. Second, the question of how the model actually becomes operationalized and used will be explored. Finally, some of the critical questions that must be dealt with at different stages in the model will identified.

A MODEL OF THE DATA-COLLECTION/FEEDBACK CYCLE

Underlying the many different ways of using data for organizational change is an implicit model of the process for using data. In its simplest form, any data-based method involves a means for collection of data, an approach to interpreting and analyzing the information, and a method for feeding the data back to relevant individuals or groups. While approaches on how to perform each of these activities vary, all of them assume that some sequence of collection, analysis, and feedback will occur, as they are the core activities of any data-based method. However, there are other activities which should also be included as parts of this sequence.

Before data collection begins there should be planning for the data's use. The client organization and individuals in that organization should have a clear understanding of what type of data will be collected, how data will be analyzed, and how it will be fed back. Data feedback in and of itself may bring about only limited change. The process of using data after it has been fed back is important. The degree to which the individuals or groups receiving feedback use the information for problem solving and goal setting determines the ultimate effects of the data on behavior. Therefore another phase should be added to the cycle to include those activities undertaken as follow-up to the actual feedback of data.

The data-collection/feedback cycle therefore includes five specific stages of activity (see Figure 3.1):

1. *Planning to use data.* During this stage the client system makes the decision to proceed with data collection, with an understand-

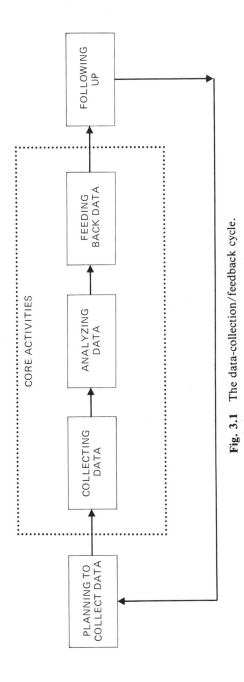

Fig. 3.1   The data-collection/feedback cycle.

ing of the implications of that decision for feedback and ultimate use of the data. In this stage specific plans are also formulated for data collection and use.

2. *Collecting data.* The activity here involves the planned gathering of information about the client system.

3. *Analyzing data.* In some manner the raw data (that is, the observations and collected information) need to be interpreted and prepared in some meaningful and usable form.

4. *Feeding back data.* The interpreted or organized data must be fed back to the client system to check on its validity and to initiate change activities.

5. *Following up.* This stage involves those activities designed to build on the feedback experience so that meaningful change can be brought about.

As a result of follow-up activities, additional or repeated data collections may be needed; in such cases, the cycle begins again with a repetition in some form of the preparation stage before additional data collection is initiated.

These five stages of activity form a model for using data-based methods. The model is a general one, but it is applicable to a whole variety of situations. Data collection and feedback at the individual, group, or organizational level include these elements. This can be illustrated by examples of these levels.

At the individual level, the performance appraisal process, if conducted effectively, gives us a good example of data-collection/feedback cycle. When a new subordinate begins work for a manager, the first thing the manager should do is provide as clear a picture as possible of the subordinate's functions, responsibilities, and goals. The manager should also provide the subordinate with information about performance measures and standards, as well as the way in which performance will be evaluated. Thus the "ground rules" for data collection and usage are worked out ahead of time. As the subordinate works, the manager collects data about the subordinate's behavior and performance. Based on that data, as well as on other factors (for example, how conditions have changed since the standards and goals were set), the manager makes a tentative interpretation of the subordinate's performance. Finally, the manager and the subordinate sit down to review the performance data and to discuss its validity and meaning, as well as its implications for the future. They may agree that things are going well or they may identify some additional development needs (for example, training) for the subordinate.

An example at the group level can be seen in a situation where a consultant has been asked to work with a group or team to help improve the processes of working together. As a first step, the consultant clarifies his or her role and relationship with the group and describes a little of what he or she will be doing (planning). Next the consultant observes the group as it works together and may also interview individuals regarding their feelings about the group and perceptions of how well the group works (collection). Based on these observations the consultant then begins to form a picture of the patterns of behavior that exist in the group and the kinds of behavior that prevent the group from getting its work done. In a sense there is a comparison between actual processes in the group and some model of how this group should be working (analysis). The consultant may describe what has been observed, check this observation for validity, and begin to stimulate the group to become aware of its process (feedback). This collection-analysis-feedback may occur within a few minutes in the form of a single process intervention or it may occur over a longer period of time leading to a more lengthy and detailed feedback period. Finally, the consultant continues work with the group members to help them develop their own capability to examine and problem-solve around process issues (follow up).

These two examples are very different; however, they both include the basic activities of planning, collection, analysis, feedback, and follow-up. As can be seen in Table 3.1, both situations share a common sequence of events. Similarly, at the organizational level of analysis, it is possible to identify these stages. In Table 3.2, for example, the major events of the three cases described in Chapter 2 are given within the framework of the data-collection/feedback cycle.

Table 3.1

Examples of the data-collection/feedback cycle
at the individual and group levels.

Situation	Supervisor conducts performance appraisal	Consultant works with a group
Planning to use data	Supervisor clarifies subordinate's functions, responsibilities, and goals. Sets "ground rules" for performance measurement and evaluation.	Group (or team) asks for help in working together. Group and consultant agree on the consultant's role.
Collecting data	Supervisor observes and records performance of subordinate.	Consultant observes interactions of group.
Analyzing data	Supervisor compares actual performance vs. standards and checks to see if conditions have changed.	Consultant compares actual process in group with ideal processes and attempts to identify patterns of behavior.
Feeding back data	Supervisor shares data and interpretations with subordinate. They discuss validity and implications of performance data.	Consultant describes aspects of group process as observed. Checks observations for accuracy and stimulates discussion of process issues.
Following up	Plans are jointly developed for remediation—training or new job assignments.	Consultant continues to work with group and helps group to develop its own capability to observe and give feedback on its process.

Table 3.2
Major events of three case studies classified in the
data-collection/feedback cycle.

	Winfield School District	Northeastern Hospital	People's National Bank
Planning to use data	Consultant prepares proposal, conducts orientation sessions, sets up steering committees.	Consultant team negotiates with the executive committee, then holds meetings with all staff.	Research team meets with managers and works with an internal task force to design feedback system.
Collecting data	Questionnaires are administered in different schools.	Interviews, questionnaires, observations, and records are used as data sources over several months.	Questionnaires and performance data are collected monthly by the feedback system.
Analyzing data	Consultant does basic analysis and preparation of raw data.	Consultants do entire analysis of data collected in order to prepare a report.	Feedback system does basic aggregation of data but no interpretation.
Feeding back data	Questionnaire results are given back in formal work groups, starting from the top and working down.	Formal feedback sessions are held with large (50-60) groups of employees. A report is read to the group by the consultants.	Computer print-outs are provided to each branch and monthly meetings are held to work with the data.
Following-up	Action plans are developed and implemented. A second survey keeps the process going.	The executive committee considers the recommendations of the consultants (little happens).	Specific changes suggested in the meetings are implemented. Continued collection and feedback keep the process going.

Given the applicability of this model to several different levels of analysis, the emphasis from here on will be on the data-collection/feedback cycle at the organizational level, rather than at the group or individual level. There are several reasons for this choice. First, the organizational level is obviously the most complex. Therefore focusing on that level will enable us to deal with problems that subsume the individual and group-level problems. Given the applicability of the model to all three levels, it is most economical to deal with the most complex level of analysis. Second, there already exist a number of different discussions of the issue of providing individual feedback (Schein and Bennis, 1963; Walton, 1969) and the approaches to using feedback at the group level (Schein, 1969; Beckhard, 1969). There is not, however, much detailed information concerning the issues and approaches to feedback and data-based change at the organizational level. Thus the focus will be on organizational-level processes and issues, with the assumption that most of what is said will also be applicable in some form to the individual and group situations. At the organizational level, many examples will be drawn from one specific data-based method—survey feedback. This is done because survey feedback (the use of employee attitude and perception questionnaires for collection and feedback) is probably the most widely used organizational-level collection and feedback method. As will be pointed out, however, it is not the only data-based method nor is it necessarily the best method in all situations.

HOW THE DATA-COLLECTION/
FEEDBACK CYCLE ACTUALLY OCCURS

The data-collection/feedback model as presented in the previous section is a straightforward, rational, step-by-step process. As can be seen in Fig. 3.1, each stage is in a specified order, and each step seems to be of equal importance. Actually, this is a distorted picture. The order in which these steps proceed is, in reality, quite different from the neat sequential model presented earlier.

The process of using data for organization development might better be pictured as shown in Fig. 3.2. Three activities—the feedback, the activities that lead to the feedback, and the planning process—are of major importance and should relate to one another, based on the

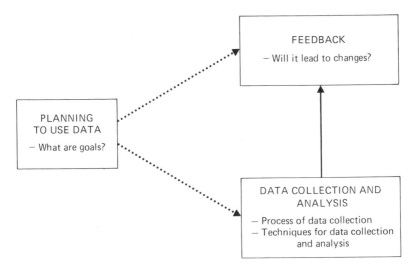

Fig. 3.2 Operationalizing the data-collection/analysis cycle.

fact that feedback is the most important part of the whole data-based cycle. Major and lasting change (as we shall see in the following chapters) comes about largely through feedback, as opposed to the other activities in the cycle. The real payoff from using data-based methods comes when the data are returned to individuals in the organization and problem solving begins.

Of course, the occurrence of feedback does not assure that change will come about. Whether feedback leads to change is determined by the way in which feedback data are given and worked with. It is also determined by the nature of the events that lead to the feedback. Thus all collection-feedback activities should work toward feedback if the data are to be successfully used.

In particular (see Fig. 3.2), the success of data feedback is greatly influenced by the other activities in the data-collection/feedback cycle, such as the processes used to collect data and the specific techniques of data collection and analysis. If the wrong data are collected, if data are inadequately analyzed, or if the process of collection creates suspicion and anxiety, then successful feedback will be very difficult to obtain. Conversely, data-collection methods, which generate interest and thought about important problems, collection techniques which enable the gathering of useful and important data, and analysis which enables a meaningful interpretation of those data, can greatly aid feedback.

A final, yet extremely important link in this process is planning. Given that feedback is the major component for creating change in the cycle and given that other activities are important because they lead to feedback, the planning process must address the following questions:

1. What are the goals for the data-based activities? What do we want to happen? What do we want to change?

2. In order to make those changes occur, what kind of feedback do we envision?

3. In order for desired feedback activities to occur, what kinds of information should be collected? How will it be collected? How will it be analyzed?

4. In order for the whole process of collection-feedback-change to occur, what other decisions need to be made (for example, who will control the data, who will run feedback meetings, etc.)?

As seen from the sequence of these questions, preparing to use data in an organization is not as straightforward as the orderly data-collection/feedback cycle previously presented. The first concern must be the ultimate goals of the data-based activities and the type of feedback activities needed to achieve those goals. Planning should work "backwards" from feedback, by determining what factors are needed to make feedback effective.

Two earlier case studies illustrated the importance of planning with the feedback component clearly in mind. In the Winfield School District case, the consultant carefully planned for the clarification of project goals and was in agreement with management on the kind of feedback that would ultimately occur. Thus the consultant and the relevant power groups (such as management and the teachers' council) had the same view of how the feedback process would appear. Only then did they begin to work on determining what type of data to collect, how to collect it, and how to analyze it. Thus the feedback process occurred as planned and led to the beginning of significant changes in that organization.

In contrast, the consultants and management in the Northestern Hospital case never clearly defined what the ultimate project goals might be in anything other than vague terms. The issue of feedback was left partially unresolved, to be dealt with in detail only after the results were in. At that point, a surprised and threatened management prevented the consultants from creating a meaningful feedback experience. Thus despite the use of effective data-collection and analysis methods, the consultants failed to facilitate change in the organization. Instead of planning only for collection and analysis, they should have reached an agreement with management concerning goals and the nature of the feedback process.

Despite the actual use of a nonlinear approach to using data-based methods (starting with feedback and working backwards in the cycle), the straightforward sequential model (as seen in Figure 3.1) will continue to be used. The subsequent discussions of data-based methods will, for the most part, be ordered sequentially, trusting that those who actually use data-based methods will remember that the straightforward model is somewhat of an oversimplication.

MAJOR IMPLEMENTATION CONCERNS

The implementation of the data-collection/feedback cycle is not a simple process. At each step, the change agent and the organization must deal with a number of important questions if the ultimate goals of effective feedback and change are to be achieved.

In Table 3.3 a number of important implementation concerns have been listed. First, several questions must be considered while planning how to use data. As we saw in the Winfield and Northeastern cases, how the data-based cycle begins and the expectations that are created early in the process are important. There is a need to establish a clear relationship between the client organization and the consultant. The ultimate goals and expectations of each must in some way be specified, perhaps in a contract. Critical decisions must be made concerning the kind of data to be collected, how those data will be collected, and how they will be used. Some particularly important questions are: Who is to control or influence the data-based activities? Will it be a management project or will others participate in making

Table 3.3
Major implementation concerns

Planning to use data	Building a clear-cut relationship between client and consultant; developing a contract.
	Planning for data collection—what kind of data to collect and how to collect it.
	Planning how data will be used and by whom.
	Planning for data-based activity evaluation.
The process of collecting data	What are the goals of data collection?
	What are the process issues in data collection? What effects will data gathering have?
Techniques for collecting and analyzing data?	What are the most appropriate data collection methods?
	What tools, techniques, and resources can be used to understand what the data mean once collected?
Feedback of data and follow-up	What is effective feedback?
	How can data be effectively presented?
	What are the problems in feedback meetings and how can they be dealt with?
	How can meetings and other activities be structured so that feedback leads to change? What systematic approaches to feedback and follow up exist?

key decisions about data and its use? Finally, during the planning stage, some attention should be given to how the data-based change activities will be evaluated.

A second set of questions relates to the process of collecting data. The way in which data are collected can influence the feelings and motivations of people in the organization and thus affect both the validity of the data collected and the nature of the subsequent feedback activities. Some thought needs to be given to the goals of the data-collection activity: What kinds of concerns may be raised when collecting data? What effects will data collection have?

A third set of questions concerns the techniques used for data collection and analysis. Under what conditions are different methods of data collection (such as interviews, questionnaires, observations, and record collection) most appropriate and useful? Similarly, what tools, techniques, and resources can be used to help us understand what the data mean once they have been collected?

Finally, there are critical questions about the feedback and follow-up stages of the cycle. What is effective feedback? What kinds of information are likely to create and direct energy towards change? How can data most effectively be presented to people in organizations so that information is both meaningful and useful? A whole set of questions involves the actual forum for data feedback—the feedback meeting. What are the potential problems in these meetings and what is needed to make the meetings successful? What different approaches exist for creating successful meetings and for continued use of data after the initial feedback session?

All of these questions will be considered at length in Part III, which discusses in detail how to use data for OD. This listing, however, provides an overview of the range of concerns that must be dealt with during the various stages of the data-collection/feedback cycle in organizations.

Before moving on to a detailed discussion of implementation issues, one major remaining question needs to be considered: "Why does information change behavior?" This is a critical question. It is hard to make *good* choices among the different strategies for implementing feedback without some knowledge of why and how information in general and feedback in particular affect behavior. Thus Part 2 provides some basic concepts about information and behavior change.

PART 2
THE THEORY OF
INFORMATION AND BEHAVIOR CHANGE

4
HOW INFORMATION CHANGES BEHAVIOR

Why is information a useful change tool? How does the use of data bring about changes in the behavior of individuals, groups, and organizations? What types of data and what sets of conditions lead to what kinds of behavior changes?

These are questions which must be considered by anyone planning to use data-based methods. It is difficult to make *good* decisions about the way in which a tool (such as data) will be used without some knowledge of how the tool works. In answering these questions, however, one is faced with a problem, since most of what has been written on the use of data for interventions has not given much attention to these issues. There has been relatively little attention given to the "why" and "how" of data-based methods. As a result, little progress has been made in the development of an applied theory of information (in general) and feedback (in particular). At the same time, an examination of the work of researchers in social and organizational psychology reveals a rather large (if diffuse) body of knowledge about how information affects behavior. This research implies that the way in which information is collected and the manner in which it is fed back can have predictable effects on behavior.

This chapter presents some of this knowledge of the effects of data in what is intended as an understandable and potentially useful first statement of a model of information and change in organizations.

Armed with such a model, the manager and the change agent can begin to plan how to use data, with some ability to predict how different uses may have different effects.

BASIC CONCEPTS

Data influence and thus change behavior in two specific ways. First, information can serve to *energize* behavior; it can arouse feelings and create forces which bring about behavior changes. Information, presented to an individual, a group, or an organization, can create energy around the issues which the data describe and thus begin to motivate action. For example, the collection and feedback of questionnaire data about employee attitudes may arouse interest and create energy for management to be responsive to employee concerns, particularly if the results of the questionnaire are different from what was expected.

Second, data can be used to *direct* behavior once the motivation for action has been created. Information can be used to inform individuals, groups, or organizations of the kinds of behavior that will lead to certain outcomes or results. Returning to the example, employee responses in different parts of the questionnaire can guide management's attention toward specific problems, such as the quality of supervision or job design.

Underlying these two basic concepts is the assumption that the kind of "energizing" and "directing" of behavior that occurs is determined by the nature of the data, the collection process, the analysis, and the feedback process. Also implicit in this view is the assumption that "energizing" behavior is a prerequisite to "directing" behavior. Information cannot bring about change in the absence of the motivation to change.

Given this general view of how information changes behavior, we will focus on two specific issues and attempt to define some conceptual models in these areas. First, we will consider how the *collection of data* creates energy and, to a lesser extent, directs energy. Second, we will look at the issue of *feedback,* and consider how feedback both energizes and directs behavior. Throughout this discussion we will refer to the effects of information on behavior at multiple levels. While the easiest approach would be to consider the effects of feedback on one individual or a small group of people, the models should also be applicable to the behavior of the entire organization as it too reacts to information. In a final section of this chapter, we will attempt to explain some general *implications* of the theory for the change agent.

HOW THE COLLECTION
OF DATA INFLUENCES BEHAVIOR

Collection effects occur because even the simple act of collecting information in an organization can arouse and direct energy. Much of the knowledge about how measurement affects behavior comes from studies of control systems and control processes in organizations from a behavioral perspective (Lawler & Rhode, 1976; Newman, 1975). This work has begun to clarify how the collecting of data can bring about certain types of behavior changes. Specifically, it indicates that data collection (or measurement) generates energy around the activities or behavior being measured; that the amount of energy generated depends upon various factors surrounding the collection; and that the direction of that energy can also be influenced.

Measurement Generates Energy

Studies have indicated that individuals, groups, and organizations tend to concentrate their energies and resources in those areas where data are collected, as opposed to those areas where there is no measurement or data collection (Cammann, 1974). Examples of this effect of collection abound. A bank branch manager directs effort into generating loan volume (measured) while ignoring the task of developing managers in his or her staff (unmeasured). A nursing team puts more effort into filling out activity reports (measured) than into patient education (unmeasured). Similarly, an organization pays more attention to its return on invested capital (measured) than its return on human investment (unmeasured).

Why does this generation of energy occur? Why do individuals and groups concentrate their efforts in measured areas? Part of the answer can be found in an understanding of some basic concepts of motivation. Most people who study behavior in organizations agree that much of an individual's behavior is determined by his or her perceptions of the possible rewards or punishments which may result from behavior (Lawler, 1973). Although there are a number of different theories explaining how this occurs, there is general agreement that individuals will choose to perform those behaviors which they see as leading to the best combination of favorable or desirable outcomes.

Data collection generates energy because it affects perceptions of how the behavior being measured may be rewarded or punished. This happens in several different ways.

1. *Implied Sanctions/Rewards.*   One way in which data collection generates energy is through implied sanctions or rewards. The fact that an activity is measured through data collection sends a message that some potentially powerful individual or group feels that the activity being measured is an important area. Those being measured may develop expectations that performance in the area being measured is likely to be rewarded. By implication, if the power group feels that the activity is important, then those being measured may also begin to view it as important. A clear example of this effect occurs when a supervisor begins to measure a certain aspect of a subordinate's performance. For instance, the bank branch manager may be asked by his or her superior to keep a record of all management development activities carried on by branch staff. Even in the absence of explicit rewards for performing in that area, the branch manager may devote energy to that activity because rewards or sanctions are implied by the act of measurement.

2. *Evaluation.*   Measurement generates energy because it enables and indeed facilitates evaluation. Measurement makes behavior more visible because it makes behavior observable to a wider audience. Data collection opens up possibilities for comparison where they may not have existed before. Behavior of one group can now be compared with the behavior of other groups, with the past behavior of the same group, or with some preset standard. In the bank example, management-development activities of branch managers, once measured, can be posted, distributed, or compared. These actions may further increase the energy put into this area. Again, evaluation creates the implications of rewards or sanctions and thus generates energy.

3. *Explicit Rewards.*   Data collection may be openly and explicitly tied to desired outcomes. An example occurs where pay is linked to the

measure of performance. A branch manager may find that his or her salary is affected by an evaluation of his or her performance in the area of management development. Clearly, the act of measuring in combination with a reward will serve to generate energy to change behavior.

How Much Energy is Generated?

Data-collection activities generate energy, though the amount of energy generated varies. Some data-collection activities generate great amounts of energy, while others do not generate energy at all.

Cammann and Nadler (1976), in studying control systems in organizations, have identified three factors which appear to contribute to the generation of energy. (See Fig. 4.1.) The first is the act of data collection or measurement itself; the existence of measurement activity in an area is a necessary factor for energy generation. A second factor is the perceived accuracy of the measurement; the greater the accuracy of the measurement, the more energy generated. The final factor relates to how the data are used by relevant power groups—to the individual this might represent a supervisor; to a group it might represent a supervisor or a more powerful group; to the organization it might represent some outside group (for example, the

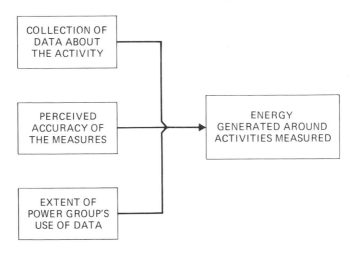

Fig. 4.1 Factors contributing to generation of energy by data collection.

government, shareholders, etc.) The key issue is the importance ascribed to the data by the relevant power groups. The greater the ascribed importance, the greater the probability of rewards and sanctions based on the data; thus the greater the amount of energy generated.

Perception is obviously a key factor in this model of collection effects. Individuals whose activities are being measured are motivated to behave in certain ways because they *perceive* that data collection may affect their ability to obtain desired outcomes. The amount of energy or motivation generated depends on whether these individuals perceive their activities as being measured, how accurate the measures are perceived to be, and how much importance powerful groups or individuals are perceived to attribute to the data.

Where is Energy Directed?

The collection-effects model as developed so far describes how energy is generated. It does not address the issue of what type of energy is generated or how that energy is directed. Control-systems research reveals that data collection can produce productive and nonproductive energy—that is, data collection can generate energy directed toward "doing a better job" on the activities or behavior being measured, but it can also generate energy toward changing the data without actually improving performance.

Data collection may generate increased effort, more effective problem-solving, or greater application of resources to those activities being measured. This is often the desired result of data collection. A change agent, for example, would probably anticipate such effects from data collection. In particular, the collection of data about interpersonal processes in an organization might have several positive effects. For instance, supervisors might see such data collection as a message concerning the importance of interpersonal processes and might begin to put more effort into improving process in their work groups. Similarly, the collection of such data might stimulate groups to examine issues which are the subject of data collection and do some problem solving around these issues. Finally, data collection might generate an interest in more fully understanding the nature of the data collected and would thus generate positive motivation to use the feedback.

Most data-collection activity is designed to create positively directed energy. In some cases, the collector may ignore the collection effects completely. Unfortunately, collection cannot be assumed to be a benign act, with either nonexistent or positive effects. Data collection can generate energy directed toward nonproductive or counterproductive activity. Counterproductive activity can take many different forms (Argyris, 1952).

First, there may be a *reduction in the availability of valid information*. For example, employees may decline to be interviewed or may refuse to fill out a questionnaire or may choose to withhold information because they feel that nothing positive will result from giving valid information to a change agent.

Second, data collection may result in *false or misleading information*. Individuals often provide information which makes them "look good" or they may present false data in order to sabotage the collection activities, which they see as leading to undesirable outcomes. For example, when a process observer is present, a group may behave in a manner to prevent negative data from arising. Others might purposely give inaccurate responses on a questionnaire in order to destroy the usefulness of the survey.

Third, data collection may lead to *misdirected energy*. That is, individuals become overly concerned with the activities that are being measured to the exclusion of other activities (which may be equally important). Individuals may also become overly concerned with "numbers" and may behave in ways which change the data, but little else. In one survey-feedback situation, for example, employees found themselves subjected to a great deal of pressure and harassment after the results of an initial survey indicated dissatisfaction with a supervisor. According to one of the employees, when the next survey round occured, they rated the supervisor higher than they did before to "get him off our backs." This represents a concern for numbers and their consequences, rather than a change in supervisory behavior. The control-systems literature contains many examples of misdirected energy, especially situations where one number (for example, production cost) is increased at the expense of another critical factor (for example, delivery time or product quality).

Finally, data collection may encourage individuals to engage in *defensive behavior*. Specifically, if employees anticipate that data collection may bring negative or highly threatening information to the surface, they may be motivated by the act of collection itself to discredit the data or its significance. Thus a data-collection effort might be met with comments like the following: "Consultants only tell us what we already know." "These change agents always talk with the malcontents or agitators and ignore the mass of employees." "Surveys never give an accurate picture of the real problems." All of these statements are defenses against possibly threatening information; they attempt to discredit information sources in advance.

What Determines the Direction of Energy Generated?

Data collection can generate different kinds of energy and can direct it in very different ways. As mentioned above, factors such as the presence of measures, the perceived accuracy of measures, and the importance attributed to data by power groups are critical in determining how much energy will be generated by data collection. Several questions remain unanswered, however. What determines the direction of the energy generated? What makes the difference between data collection that generates productive energy and data collection that generates counterproductive energy?

Much of the control-systems research indicates that the perceptions people have *at the time of data collection* about possible uses of the data *in the future* affect the direction of energy (Cammann, 1974; Nadler, Mirvis, and Cammann, 1976). A major determinant of the direction of energy is the quality of usage by the relevant power group (be it an outside group, another group within the organization, or an individual such as a supervisor or manager). Those individuals who are being measured develop expectations about how the power group or individual will use the data; these expectations are based on past experience, as well as the explicit "contract" that may exist with the data collectors. Based on these expectations, individuals or groups may direct their energy in different ways. For example, a group which expects its manager to use the data in an open and nonevaluative manner to collectively identify and solve problems may be motivated to provide accurate information and to work with that information when it is fed back. On the other hand, a group which expects its manager to use the data in a punitive manner may choose to distort the data and/or deny its accuracy before it is fed back in order to avoid the expected undesirable outcomes.

Specifically, different patterns of usage seem to be associated with different direction of energy. One pattern of usage has been labeled "reactive control." Here the power group uses the data to react to past behavior. Data are used evaluatively and sometimes punitively; rewards are tied to changes in the data. There are some situations where such a strategy might be useful. In particular such a strategy might work in the context of a nonparticipative organization —where the manager is highly directive, where the employees have little desire for increased autonomy or participation, and where extensive foolproof measures of performance exist. In most cases, however, this strategy would lead to the direction of energy in nonproductive directions. In a number of studies, managers' use of data reactively has been observed as resulting in defensive behavior, falsification of data. and misdirected energies (Cammann, 1974).

Another strategy, that of using data to work on future behavior rather than punishing or evaluating past behavior, is associated with different responses. Using data *proactively* includes the use of information for problem identification and problem solving and, in particular, for goal setting. Thus the focus of data use is on more effective behavior in the future, rather than on ineffective behavior in the past. This strategy directs energy in productive directions, and it seems to motivate employees to provide valid information to the data collectors. It generates energy toward making use of the information in solving both organizational and individual problems.

A Model of Collection Effects

What emerges from this discussion of the effects of collecting data is a model which shows how data collection can motivate and direct behavior in organizational settings (see Fig. 4.2). The presence of accurate measures (with attributed importance) creates expectations that the data collection will affect the nature of rewards or sanctions obtained as a result of behavior. This in turn leads to the generation of energy related to the behaviors or activities being measured. At the same time, current and previous patterns of usage of the data by power groups or individuals also create expectations about the possible consequences of data collection. Depending on what these expectations are, energy will be directed toward productive behavior or toward counterproductive behavior.

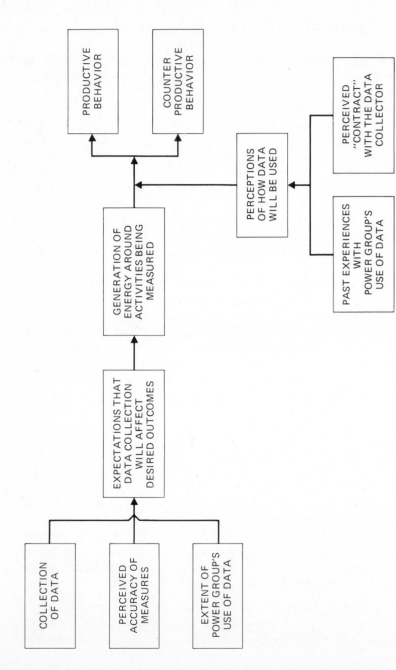

Fig. 4.2   A model of the effects of data collection on behavior.

HOW DATA FEEDBACK INFLUENCES BEHAVIOR

As we have presented it, any data-based method includes three basic components: collection, analysis, and feedback. Two of these, collection and feedback, have direct effects upon behavior. In the discussion of collection effects, we saw that collecting information can bring about behavior change because individuals and groups have expectations about the possible consequences of data collection. These expectations, based on past experiences with data collection or change agents, lead to the generation and direction of energy. While collection effects are very significant, the most potent and direct use of data for change is to give the information back in some form to the organization's members. *This process of giving data back for the purpose of bringing about change is called feedback.*

Feedback can create changes in the behavior of individuals, groups, or organizations because it both energizes (i.e., motivates) and directs behavior. To facilitate an understanding of how this is accomplished, several specific questions will be examined. First, there is a need to more clearly define the term "feedback." A second concern is to identify a number of feedback functions and the way in which they bring about behavior change. Third, is the task of identifying those parts of the feedback process that can affect the generation and direction of energy. Based on these discussions, a general model of feedback effects will be constructed.

What is Feedback?

Feedback as a concept was developed in the 1940s and 1950s, when scientists began looking at the world in terms of systems models. They were interested in the nature of systems, the applicability of systems models to both the physical and social world, and the use of systems concepts for specific applications.

The term "feedback" was introduced into general usage by Wiener (1948; 1950) in his formulations of an approach called *cybernetic theory*. In discussing the basic concepts describing a mechanical system Wiener (1950) writes:

> For any machine subject to a varied external environment to act effectively, it is necessary that information concerning the results of its own action be furnished to it . . . This control of a machine

on the basis of its actual performance rather than its expected performance is known as feedback.

Feedback is thus defined as information regarding actual performance or the results of the activities of a system. Not all information is feedback; only information which is used to control the future functioning of the system is considered feedback. This basic view of feedback is illustrated in Fig. 4.3. A system is a mechanism which obtains input from a larger environment, subjects the input to a transformation process, and then produces output.

In this model, feedback is a controlling information channel which connects the system's output with its input. Specifically, a feedback loop is an information channel that translates the measure of the output of a system into a signal which can then control the input or the transformation processes. Feedback is thus information about the system output which controls the system functioning. Wiener (1950) calls feedback "the property of being able to adjust future conduct by past performance."

As the systems-model concept developed in the 50's and 60's, it became evident that the concept of systems (in general) and feedback (in particular) could be applied to social systems as well as to physical or mechanical systems. In the social system, however, the process of using system-output information to change system functioning is somewhat more complex than in the mechanical model. Wiener (1950) suggests this:

> Feedback is a method of controlling a system by reinserting into it the results of its past performance. If those results are merely

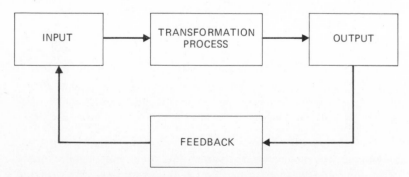

Fig. 4.3 The basic systems feedback model.

used as numerical data for the criticism of the system and its regulation, we have the simple feedback of the control engineers. If, however, the information which proceeds backward from performance is able to change the general method and pattern of performance, we have a process which may well be called learning.

This view of the learning function of feedback in a social system has two major implications. First, feedback may have broader effects than those of just changing the input of a system. Feedback may also have an impact on the processes by which the output is produced. Feedback can be more than just a device to regulate flows through the system—it can be a way to change how the system does its work.

Second, the issue of option is introduced—feedback can be used in different ways. This is significant since the social scientist's use of the feedback concept has been different from that of the physical scientist's. The social science concept of feedback has become synonymous with the term "knowledge of results," including any information about output even though it may not control an input or a transformation process. Potential feedback information may exist, but in many cases the system may not exercise the option of using the data. It is a much less automatic process.

The systems theory concept became widespread in the 60's and began to influence the thinking and writing done about formal work organizations. Once again, the feedback concept went through a process of further definition. In particular, many theorists talked about the important role feedback plays in helping organizations to continually correct errors and adapt to a changing environment. An example of such thinking (Katz and Kahn, 1966) follows:

> . . . The feedback principle has to do with information input which is a special kind of energic importation, a kind of signal to the system about environmental conditions and about the functioning of the system in relation to its environment. The feedback of such information enables the system to correct for its own malfunctioning or for changes in the environment, and thus maintain a steady state . . .

Note that feedback *enables* system correction rather than automatically bringing it about. This point is important since in organizations potential feedback information can exist but may be ignored. In the broad view, this inadequate use of feedback information by organizations is the underlying rationale for organization development. The change agent performs the critical function of collecting data and facilitating its use through the feedback process so that organizations can correct malfunctions, adapt to changes in the environment (either internal or external to the organization), and hopefully learn.

From this discussion we can extract a few major points, which will provide a basic working definition and an understanding of the concept of feedback in organizations:

1. Feedback is a basic component of self-regulating systems.

2. In its most precise form, feedback is information about the output of a system which controls the system input or transformation processes.

3. In its broader forms, feedback is any information about the system functioning which has the potential of being used to change the operation of the system.

4. Viewing organizations as open systems, feedback is a necessary component, enabling the correction of errors, the adaptation to environmental change, and learning.

5. Since in social systems such as work organizations feedback does not automatically create change in the system operation, the process of obtaining, interpreting, and using feedback information is important.

6. Since organizations often ignore feedback or do not make an effort to use feedback effectively, organization development activities serve an important function of facilitating feedback processes, thus helping organizations to correct errors, adapt, learn, and grow.

How Feedback Changes Behavior

Examining feedback at the system or organizational level provides a straightforward view of how feedback changes behavior. Feedback is an error correction device which enables a system to adapt over time. When we begin to look at groups and individuals, however, we find that the simple error-correction model is not adequate for explaining how different kinds of feedback bring about different kinds of behavior.

There has been extensive research on how feedback affects the behavior of individuals (Ammons, 1956; Annett, 1969). Most of the work, however, at both the individual and group level has been highly theoretical and, with a few exceptions, not oriented toward developing useful models for practitioners in organizations. It is possible, however, to extract from this work some general patterns of findings which may say something meaningful to the practitioner desiring to use feedback as an intervention tool.

Feedback affects behavior, by performing two different types of functions, in a manner similar to the way data collection affects behavior (Locke, Cartledge and Koeppel, 1968). First, feedback serves to create or generate energy. This generation of energy is frequently called the *motivating function* of feedback. Second, feedback serves to direct behavior where motivation already exists. This *directing function* is to a large extent similar to the error-correction model developed by the systems theorists.

There are a number of different ways in which feedback information serves a motivating or directing function. Table 4.1 provides a summary of the feedback mechanisms along with a listing of some critical conditions necessary for each mechanism to work. The first three conditions explain different ways in which feedback creates energy and thus motivates behavior. The last two conditions describe ways in which feedback serves to direct behavior where motivation already exists.

1. *Motivating Behavior by Disconfirmation.* Feedback has the potential for motivating and thus changing behavior by providing information which is inconsistent with the perceptions or beliefs of individuals or groups. The creation of inconsistent perceptions can arouse or create anxiety. Thus be creating a situation where the performer (the individual or group who is the target of the feedback) experiences inconsistent perceptions, feedback can motivate behavior toward resolution of the inconsistency (Peak, 1955; Schein and Bennis, 1965). Such data can be disconfirming or can provide lack of confirmation for existing beliefs.

In order for feedback to change behavior through this mechanism, the data must be perceived as valid and accurate. If the

Table 4.1
How feedback affects group and individual performance.

	Feedback function	*How the mechanism works*	*Necessary conditions*
Motivating function	Disconfirmation	Feedback motivates behavior by providing information that presents inconsistent perceptions	Data must be perceived as accurate Conditions must be present to prevent defensive behavior
	Internal-reward expectancies	Feedback motivates behavior by setting up expectations that behavior will lead to feedback, which in itself generates positive feelings in the individual or group. In addition, it provides a standard against which goals can be set	Level of behavior to obtain favorable feedback must be attainable Task must be challenging so that attainment is desirable Feedback must include some comparison data as a standard Conditions must be present to facilitate goal-setting
	External-reward expectancies	Feedback motivates behavior by setting up expectations that behavior will lead to feedback which in turn will lead to the attainment of other valued rewards from the environment	Level of behavior to obtain rewards must be attainable Instrumentality of feedback for rewards must be high Rewards must be valued ones

	Feedback function	How the mechanism works	Necessary conditions
Directing function	Cueing	Feedback calls attention to errors which can be corrected through known and established routines of behavior	Feedback must be specific Correction routines must be clear and understood
	Learning	Feedback calls attention to errors where correction behavior has not yet been identified and thus must be discovered	Feedback should be on process as well as outcome variables Feedback should include models of effective behavior Group or individual must have effective search routines

data are seen as inaccurate and therefore not believable, then the inconsistent perception will not create motivation. There is no reason to be concerned if new but inaccurate data are not consistent with other perceptions or beliefs. Second, the conditions surrounding the feedback process should support the nonthreatening use of data for identifying and solving problems. Schein and Bennis (1965) call this *psychological safety*. In the absence of constructive uses for energy, inconsistent perceptions can motivate defensive behavior. One way of dealing with the anxiety created by the inconsistent perceptions is to deny the validity of new data, distort its meaning, belittle its significance, etc.

An example of the disconfirmation mechanism can be seen in the response of a top management group who met with a consultant to obtain the results of a long-term diagnostic effort. The management group had begun the project with a certain degree of complacency, reflected in comments such as, "We know what our problems are," or "Everything is under control." Many group members showed very little enthusiasm for the consulting project. The consultant spent 45 minutes presenting an overview of the diagnosis, feeding back key data collected along with some tentative interpretations. During and following the feedback presentation, management group members became very excited (and some very agitated) about the findings. After the discussion, the meeting concluded with specific plans for future action, additional feedback, and group meetings. Obviously, a great deal of energy had been created by the presentation of the diagnostic report.

2. *Motivating Behavior by Creating Extrinsic Reward Expectancies.*   One way in which information affects or changes behavior is that it alters the perceptions that certain activity will lead to desired outcomes (Lawler, 1973). Feedback may motivate behavior changes, where the perception exists that changes in feedback data will lead to changes in the rewards or sanctions which will be received (from the organization, environment, coworkers, etc.). The feedback process creates the expectation that behavior will lead to feedback and feedback will lead to reward. Feedback becomes instrumental for the attainment of desired outcomes.

For feedback to work as an external motivator and change tool, certain conditions must be present. First, the level of performance necessary to obtain favorable feedback and rewards must be seen as attainable by the group or individuals who are the target of the behavior change. Next, a clear link must be established between receiving feedback and receiving rewards. Finally, the outcome (reward or sanction) must have some value for the performer.

> The value of feedback as a change mechanism linked to external rewards is illustrated in the PNB case, where work groups began to receive periodic feedback of loan volume as part of a larger feedback intervention. Knowing that loan volume was related to salary increase, the group became extremely motivated to raise the loan volume figure, and began discussing ways to increase loan volume (and by implication to increase individual earnings).

3. *Motivating Behavior by Creating Internal Reward Expectancies.*   Although feedback is frequently valued since it is seen as leading to desired rewards provided by the organization or the environment, feedback frequently may be a reward in itself. Feedback may

be a desired outcome because it signals to the group or individual that the behavior performed is of a good quality, that performance is favorable relative to other groups, or, conversely, that performance is poor. In either case the feedback itself is a source of rewards or sanctions.

Research indicates that the internal-motivation effects of feedback come about through goal setting. Feedback is an integral part of the process by which individuals choose the goals which they hope to achieve and for which they exert energy to attain. Much of the research on goal setting and motivation indicates that feedback is an inherent and thus necessary part of the goal-setting process (Zander, 1971). Similarly, goal setting is necessary for obtaining the feedback to bring about changes in motivation (Locke, Cartledge, and Koeppel, 1968). Feedback is an important part of goal setting, since it is difficult to set goals for the future in the absence of knowledge about performance in the past and how that performance compares with some standard.

Feedback works as an internal motivator when several conditions are present. The level of behavior needed to obtain favorable feedback must be perceived as attainable by the performer. If the level of performance needed to obtain favorable feedback is too high, then the performer may become frustrated. On the other hand, the task must be challenging enough so that the performer will have positive feelings upon accomplishment and when receiving feedback; if this is not the case, feedback may be seen as relatively meaningless data on performance of a task which has little value or meaning.

In addition, for feedback to motivate through goal setting, the data must include some form of comparison data or standard so that a basis or bench mark for setting future goals can be obtained. More importantly, the feedback process must provide an opportunity to set goals and must facilitate goal setting, since feedback without goal setting may not lead to behavior changes. It is important to remember that feedback can affect motivation and behavior in different ways, positively as well as negatively. Feedback that performance was poor relative to a goal, for example, may encourage a lowering of aspiration levels.

The value of feedback as an internal motivator can be seen in the following example. A medical center had an internal consultant develop and implement a weekly survey of patient attitudes and perceived quality of care. The results of this survey were fed back to staff members in the different patient-care units on a regular basis. In one particular unit, a great interest developed in the patient survey and staff members began working on ways to improve the quality of care. Over a period of time, the staff (in group meetings) set goals in terms of the survey. They decided to attempt to improve conditions in the unit so that, after three months, the average patient survey score would have improved one full point (a seven point scale was used). Each week the group worked on developing new ideas, solving problems, and monitoring their progress in the survey results. The new measure and goal-setting process that developed became a powerful motivator.

4. *Directing Behavior by Cueing.*   Motivation, or the creation of energy, causes the first three mechanisms to work. Feedback motivates certain behavior, because it affects the perceptions of individuals about external or internal rewards. Feedback can also change behavior in a very different way. Assuming that energy already exists, feedback is valuable as a guide or an error-correction device.

Feedback serves a directing function through *cueing* (Annett, 1969). Feedback information provides the performer with cues that indicate whether an activity is proceeding well or poorly as compared to some standard. The cueing mechanism assumes that the performer has an explicit, obvious, and often predetermined plan of action for correction of behavior after receiving feedback which indicates the problems. A classic example of cueing effects is given in the case of a truck driver who receives visual feedback cues that the truck is moving out of its lane and onto the shoulder of the highway. The truck driver responds to the feedback cue by turning the steering wheel, correcting the problem, and simultaneously receiving visual feedback cues that the truck is now in the proper lane.

Again, several conditions must be present for feedback to serve as an effective cueing device for behavior change. First, the feedback must be specific. Nonspecific feedback can cue a variety of responses, some of which may be incorrect. Second, using feedback for cueing assumes that the correct behavior routines are clear and either well known to the performer or so obvious that the performer would immediately perceive the appropriate correction. In the absence of these conditions, cueing feedback can lead to frustration, inappropriate responses, and failure to correct problems. Cueing as a directing mechanism works only if energy has been generated. If the motivation to work on activities indicated by cueing is not present, change does not occur.

For example, an off-site workshop was held with a representative group of employees and managers from a metropolitan post office, as part of a larger OD program. One of the activities involved small-group work on identifying organizational problems in detail, building on diagnostic data presented by a team of consultants. The small group was to feed back their problem descriptions to a larger group which would discuss possible steps of action.

One particular problem that the small group identified and reported to the larger group was the lack of orientation for new employees, who, upon starting employment with the post office, were sent to a location without any preparation. This resulted in confusion and anxiety on the part of the new workers. The small group mentioned that there was a high turnover rate during the first few days of employment.

The large group realized after receiving this information that this was a problem that could easily be solved. The group agreed to set up an orientation program for new employees which would include the requirement that new employees' supervisors go to the orientation site and personally take new employees to the work site. Thus, the large group, upon being cued to the existence of the problem, was able to implement a fairly obvious solution.

5. *Directing Behavior Through Learning.*   The image of feedback changing behavior through cueing is attractive in its simplicity and effectiveness. Unfortunately, many of the problems which occur in organizations do not have clear and obvious solutions. To expect feedback to correct behavior through cueing therefore may not always be realistic. A more complex directing mechanism is the learning situation (Annett, 1969). In the learning situation as in cueing, feedback provides the performer with information indicating whether activity is proceeding well or poorly as compared to some standard—the difference being that *the correction routine is not known or obvious.* The feedback only serves to indicate the existence of a problem; it does not indicate the solution.

Data trigger search activity which involves obtaining more information about the nature of problems and possible solutions. In a trial-and-error manner, the performer learns different correction routines, each routine involving behavior, and obtains feedback which indicates either a satisfactory response or the need to continue trials. Once accomplished and after the correction routines have been integrated into the behavior of the performer, the feedback can be used for cueing.

For the learning mechanism of feedback to bring about change in a predicted or desired direction, a number of different conditions must be present. Ideally, the feedback should provide information about process problems as well as task-performance measures. Feedback that includes only task or outcome data may not provide any indication of where to start the search for corrective action. The feedback should also include some models of desired behavior so that the individual or group will have some idea of the ultimate goal of the correction activities. While these factors are desirable, one condition is critical: the performer must have some way of beginning search routines and testing and/or evaluating alternative solutions. Frequently, this is provided by group problem-solving meetings. In the absence of conditions which facilitate (or at the least, permit) search behavior, feedback will only lead to frustration and perhaps defensive behavior as the performer confronts an indication of poor performance with no idea of how to correct it.

An example of learning effects can be seen in the activity of a joint labor-management group working with a consultant to plan interventions in an organization. Because of events not directly related to intervention (involving possible layoffs), there were bad feelings in the organization, including public threats by the union to walk out on the intervention project. These events threatened the existence of the project; however, the issue had not been directly dealt with at any of the group meetings.

At the beginning of one meeting, the consultants gave some feedback to the group, describing the types of interactions that had been observed during the past few meetings, noting the absence of some union members, and asking the group what was wrong. This started an intense discussion (which continued throughout three weekly meetings) concerning the larger organizational climate and the problems it implied for the project. The group exerted pressure for all members, and particularly representatives, to be present at these meetings. The issues were ultimately "hashed out" by the group.

At the end of the last meeting of that series, the group agreed that in the future when problems arose in the larger environment, there would be no walkouts or public threats and that each member would be committed to bringing such problems to group meetings for discussion. After receiving feedback from the consultants, the group had done problem solving, developed solutions, and developed a process for responding to problems in the future.

Factors Influencing the Direction of Behavior Change

Feedback is an effective tool for bringing about behavior change—but change in what direction? As in the case of collection effects, feedback can cause decreased performance, defensive behavior, and misdirected effort, as well as desired effects in the target groups. It is possible to identify the factors which affect the ultimate direction of behavior change (see Table 4.2). Three factors seem to be of particular importance: the characteristics of the feedback data, the characteristics of the feedback process, and the characteristics of the group or individual task structure.

Table 4.2
Factors which influence the direction of
behavior change by feedback.

Factor	Characteristics
1. Characteristics of feedback data	Specificity Evaluative content Accuracy
2. Characteristics of the feedback process	Group leadership/process Reward contingencies
3. Characteristics of the task being performed	Difficulty Interdependence

The first factor, feedback data, must be specific enough to get activity, goal setting, or search behavior going in the right direction. The data should include some evaluative content—comparisons to standards or past performance. The more accurate the data, the more likely it is to bring about change in desired directions.

The second factor, the process of using feedback data, contains two important issues. The group process and the behavior of leaders (or other powerful individuals) should emphasize participation in using the data, use in a nonpunitive manner, and goal-setting activity. In addition, for feedback to serve as an external motivator, valued rewards must be seen as contingent upon the feedback data. At the same time, connecting rewards to feedback data without developing a constructive and nonpunitive approach for using the feedback can cause defensive behavior.

The third factor is the nature and difficulty of the tasks being performed by the group or individuals. If the level of performance needed to obtain favorable feedback and/or rewards is unattainable, change in the desired direction may not occur. Similarly, tasks which are not challenging or meaningful (in the absence of external rewards) may be poor targets for motivation by feedback. In group situations, the greater the interdependence, the more emphasis that should be put on group feedback and group-level processes to work on feedback.

IMPLICATIONS FOR PRACTICE

The theory of information and change developed here is useful to the extent that it provides some guidance to the person interested in using data-based methods. In subsequent chapters, detailed discussions of data use will draw on this theory. At this point, however, a few generalizations can be made:

1. Data collection creates expectations within the organization as to how the data will be used. These expectations in turn create energy and the motivation to behave in certain ways. This motivation can be either positive or negative for the change agent, depending upon the way in which the energy is directed.

2. Before and during the collection activities the change agent should work to assure that organization members will perceive

powerful groups or individuals within the organization as being concerned about the data being collected. Where this condition is present, energy will be created by the data collection. This energy can be very useful to the change agent in getting an intervention started and in getting people motivated to use the feedback data.

3. Before and during the collection activities the change agent needs to clarify how the data being collected will be used. This is necessary because perceptions of how data will be used affect the direction of the energy created by the collection. The change agent should be able to assure organization members that the data will not be used in a reactive or punitive manner.

4. Feedback can change behavior in a number of different ways. The change agent needs to decide why he or she is using feedback, what mechanisms he or she plans to use, and what conditions must be present in order for those mechanisms to work.

5. For both motivating and directing functions, it is important that the feedback data be perceived as accurate and valid. During the feedback process it may therefore be valuable for the change agent to describe the methods of collection and analysis so that those receiving the feedback can understand where the data came from and can form judgments of the validity of the data they receive.

6. For feedback to create energy and to serve as a motivator and initiator of change, there must be some kind of reward attached to working with the data in a constructive fashion and improving performance in the area being measured. This reward can be internal (coming from achievement of goals, accomplishment of a challenging task, or resolution of inconsistent perceptions) or external (some valued outcome provided by the organization or coworkers).

7. For both motivation and direction of energy, the feedback must be used in a manner that encourages exploration and understanding of the data and its use for problem solving. Thus, the change agent's most critical task is that of assuring that the process by which the feedback is given and used is open, healthy, and effective, so that energy will be directed toward problem solving and constructive change, rather than denial, defensive behavior, or misuse of data.

5
PLANNING TO USE DATA FOR CHANGE

Many attempts to use data for organizational change fail before the first interview is conducted, before the first questionnaire is handed out, or before the first observation is made. They fail because the organization and the change agent have not adequately prepared for data collection and the events that follow. They fail because it is not clear to people what data are being collected, what will be done with the data, and why it is being collected in the first place. Failure occurs because the necessary groundwork has not been done ahead of time.

In the Northeastern Hospital case, we saw a major failure to prepare adequately for the use of data. Very specific plans were made concerning data collection; however, neither the consultants nor the client (the administrator and the executive committee) ever made clear their specific expectations and goals for the feedback activities. The client was expecting a very limited amount of feedback, with the bulk of the information being given directly to management. The consultants, on the other hand, envisioned a highly detailed, open, and participative feedback process, with employees at all levels involved in working with the data. Because the feedback stage was not specifically planned for ahead of time, each group continued in the relationship, unaware that the other group did not share their image of the feedback process until the time for feedback actually arrived. The results were undesirable for both groups. Had the feedback been planned for in advance, either an effective feedback process could have been constructed or the whole project could have been cancelled, either case being more desirable than what actually occurred.

Despite the obvious consequences of poor preparation, the failure to plan adequately is easy to understand. Data-based methods are easy to use, especially for data-collection purposes. It is not difficult to pick up a standardized questionnaire that has been used in another setting, make copies, and give them to employees to fill out. It's not uncommon to hear a consultant say, ''Let's administer the questionnaire to everyone and see what we come up with. Then we'll decide what to do with it.'' In addition, planning may raise difficult issues or problems. In the Northeastern case, the consultants might have suspected that management would not agree with their feedback design, but in the short run, it was easier to ignore the problem.

The argument will be made here that pre-collection preparation is a critical part of the process of using data-based methods. As seen in the Northeastern case, without adequate preparation many attempts to use data are doomed to failure before they ever get started. Good preparation takes time and effort, by both the client and the consultant. The payoff, however, comes in the form of useful and effective data collection, feedback, and use.

WHY IS EARLY PREPARATION IMPORTANT?

Some kind of planning and preparation must take place if data are to be used. Why is *early* and *thorough* planning so important? The answer lies, in part, in the nature of the data-collection/feedback cycle. As we saw earlier, the major effects of data use come from the feedback part of the cycle. Building on the theory of information and behavior, many of the activities that precede feedback, such as data collection, are important because they create perceptions which influence the generation and direction of energy concerning the data. It should be obvious that some early decisions, including what data to collect, how to collect it, and what analyses to perform, will have an impact on the feedback process. Thus feedback cannot be successful in stimulating and facilitating change if the wrong data are collected, if the incorrect analyses are done, or if people in the organization suspect that data will not be used constructively. The various parts of the data-collection/feedback cycle should fit together and build toward feedback. For this to happen, a number of major decisions should be made early in the process.

Other factors also argue for early and thorough planning. One factor is that data may become more sensitive after collection and analysis. Once the data have been collected and people sense what kinds of information will be revealed in feedback, they begin to view the feedback process in light of self-interests. For example, the department manager who finds that feedback data will reflect poorly on the functioning of his or her department may become hesitant about having the data widely distributed. The point is that early in the data-collection/feedback cycle information is relatively benign; later in the cycle interest begins to develop as a consequence of the possible patterns of results in the data. Planning is therefore easier to do early in the cycle, rather than later.

A final factor is simply one of logistics. Collecting, analyzing, and feeding back data to large numbers of people requires that a number of decisions be made ahead of time, simply to get the collection accomplished, the data analyzed, and the information fed back in some form. Decisions have to be made about what kinds of collection techniques to use, what procedure to employ for returning data for analysis, and so on. Each of these decisions has consequences for subsequent data-based activities. For example, the decision to interview rather than use questionnaires to gather data has consequences of cost, time needed for collection, time needed for analysis, and constraints on the form of feedback. Therefore such decisions are best made early.

ISSUES IN PLANNING

In planning, the client organization and the change agent must deal with a number of critical questions. Decisions need to be made in four different areas (see Table 5.1). The first area is that of relationship building and contracting. The consultant and the organization need to make clear the nature of their relationship and to be explicit in the kinds of expectations they have. The second area involves the planning for data collection; this includes the determination of what type of data to collect and general strategies for collection. The third area involves determining how the data to be collected will be used by the organization, as well as identifying and committing the resources necessary for effective use. A final issue is that of evaluation.

Table 5.1
Critical issues in planning for data-based change.

Relationship building/contracting:	Agreeing on the goals of the change effort; determining the procedures to be used; building understanding and committment; putting expectations on paper.
Planning what data to collect:	Determining what kinds of data to collect and strategies for collection.
Planning use of the data:	Developing plans for how the data will be used for feedback and following feedback; committing resources to support effective use.
Planning evaluation:	Determining how the organization and the change agent will assess the effects of the change activities.

RELATIONSHIP BUILDING AND CONTRACTING

In the three case studies (Winfield, Northeastern, and PNB), the preliminary activities included the establishment of contacts between the consultant and the organization, discussion to see whether there was a basis for a mutually beneficial relationship, and identification of the goals and nature of the proposed consulting relationship. In each case, the consultant had relationships with different groups in an organization, such as groups of nurses, a specific high school, or several branches of a bank. These relationships existed in addition to the basic relationship between the consultants and management.

When a consultant enters an organization, he or she enters an established network of relationships between groups, individuals, and departments. If the consultant plans to use data-based methods, he or she is going to introduce potentially volatile information into that network. This means that an important question in the relationship-building phase is how will the different existing groups and individuals react to the information and the information-collection/feedback cycle. A basic concern should be, "Who will control the project—who will direct it, who will see the data, who will determine what will be done with the data, and who will ultimately benefit from the project?"

Different approaches for running the project imply very different ways of ultimately using the data, as seen in the difference between the management-directed data collection at Northeastern and the management/employee-directed processes at PNB and Winfield.

The case has been made (Schein, 1969) that the early activities of the consultant need to be congruent with the goals and values of the intervention. Thus the early decisions about how data will be collected and used should be made in a way that is consistent with the subsequent intervention activities. For example, if data are being collected to initiate a participative process of identifying and working on organizational problems, then the critical decisions about how this will happen cannot be handed down as directives from the top.

As we have seen, a number of critical issues must be dealt with during the early stages of the relationship between the consultant and the organization. Many consultants find that an explicit contract, which spells out expectations and the terms of the relationship between the consultant and the client organization, is useful. In Winfield, for example, the consultant prepared a detailed proposal which provided a framework for the relationship between him, the school district, and the individual schools. In many cases, it may be important to put the terms of the contract in writing. As in the Northeastern example, often over a period of time, perceptions of the contract change, and oral statements begin to be interpreted in different ways.

Elements of a Contract

Contracts differ in formality and detail. When preparing a contract regarding data-based change, a number of items should be included in the agreement (see Table 5.2).

The first element of a client-consultant contract should be a statement concerning the goals of the relationship. Goals may be given in very general statements such as "to improve the health and effectiveness of this organization," or in more specific statements such as "to involve the members of this organization at all levels in making the critical decisions that affect their working lives." The goals of a project represent the value positions of the consultant and the organization and they should be clearly stated in a manner that makes different members of the organization aware of them. The consultant and the client thus should agree on the purpose for their relationship and should identify the ends toward which they will be working.

Table 5.2
Basic elements of a client-consultant contract.

---

1. What are the goals of the relationship or project?

2. Who is the client and who will direct the project?

3. What kinds of data will be collected and (in general terms) how will the data be collected?

4. How will the data be used (include the procedures and resources to be used)?

5. Who will have access to the data and in what form?

6. What are the estimated time periods for the different activities?

7. How will the project be evaluated and by whom?

8. What resources will be provided by the consultant?

9. What resources will be provided by the client?

10. What process will be used to review the relationship?

The second element is that of determining who the client is. Is the client a manager or a group of managers? Is the client a group of employees or the entire organization? It is frequently not clear just who the client is, and this creates problems later on. The questions of who will have access to the data and who will ultimately use the data are related to the definition of who the client is. There are different ways of defining who the client is (Schein, 1969); however, the major concern here is "Who will run the data-collection/feedback activities within the organization?" Whoever is chosen to work with the consultant becomes the *internal partner*, who collaborates with the consultant on using data-based methods.

There are many approaches that can be used to run data-based projects; each involves a different type of internal partner. The three approaches discussed here are only a few of many possible models, but they do illustrate the range of alternatives.

One approach is the traditional *management model*. The consultant works with management and coordinates his or her activities with a member of management, a staff person who has been designated as having the internal responsibility for the project, or a group of managers. Together the consultant and management develop a plan for what type of data to collect, how to collect it, and how to conduct feedback activities. An approach of this kind was used in the Northeastern Hospital case, where the client was the administrator and the executive committee.

A second approach involves a representative group which serves as the internal partner of the consultant. This group may contain a *diagonal slice* of the organization, including people from different functional areas and different levels of the hierarchy. A number of change agents have argued for the usefulness of such groups (see, for example, Alderfer, 1975). Examples of this strategy were seen in the PNB task force and Winfield steering committees. This representative group becomes the consultant's client and works with the consultant as an internal partner to determine the type of data to be collected, how to collect it, and how to use it.

A slightly different version of the cross-sectional group is seen in a third approach—the use of joint *labor-management committees*. Recent work indicates that joint labor-management groups may be effective as the internal coordinators of interventions (National Quality of Work Center, 1975). Committees such as these have been used to manage interventions aimed at improving the quality of working life in organizations; they could also be valuable in situations where data-based methods would be used. The labor-management committee approach builds on the advantages obtained from the cross-sectional group, but it also includes the labor union, a potentially powerful force for change in organizations.

Each of these approaches has advantages and disadvantages. The greater the participation by a broad range of organizational members, the better the quality of the information obtained; resistance to data collection or intervention will also be reduced. Working with groups as clients is cumbersome and more costly than working with a single management representative, but such groups can greatly aid the consultant in his or her understanding of the nature of the organization and can help to build an effective approach to change. Again the question of congruence is important. The structure that is built to coordinate the data-based cycle should be consistent with the goals of the entire project. From a contracting perspective, it is important to decide and specify who the client is and in what form the relationship will operate (group or individual) early in the relationship.

The third contract element contains a general description of the type of data to be collected and how the data will be collected. Details of data collection usually cannot be spelled out in the contracting phase, but a general agreement should be reached. In the PNB case, a very general letter of agreement was used as a contract. After data collection had begun, one of the senior vice-presidents of the bank listened to a presentation by the consultants about questionnaires to be used and stated, "We don't believe in giving questionnaires to our employees . . . Questionnaires only cause problems and we don't think we learn very much from them." Obviously this created problems because the consultants had assumed that questionnaires would be used. The consultants then had to spend a considerable amount of time convincing this individual of the value of questionnaires. Even then he demanded the right to review all questionnaires in detail before they were administered in the bank. This type of delay occurs when the client and consultant do not reach even a general level understanding or agreement during the contracting phase regarding data collection and use.

Another question is, "How will the data be used?" Detailed plans for feedback and follow-up activities should be developed with the client over a period of time. However, a general statement concerning the use of the data should be included in the contract. The client must understand the implications of collecting and using data, and should make a firm commitment regarding the constructive use of the data. If a commitment is not made, the entire project may lead nowhere, (as in the Northeastern case), since the payoff occurs when using the data once it has been fed back. Thus some agreement should be reached on a procedure for data use, including what kinds of meetings or reports will result, who will be involved in its use, what kind of support for use will the organization provide, etc.

Though related to use, a separate issue is related to the question of *access* to the data—who will see the data, in what form, and when. One major concern here is confidentiality. In most cases, for the consultant and the organization to obtain valid information from individuals, steps must be taken to guarantee the confidentiality of individual responses. Some affirmation of confidentiality, which should be supported by safeguards concerning who has access to the data and under what conditions, should be included in the contract. Confidentiality cannot be maintained if management members, for example, have access to copies of individual questionnaires, interview notes, or process notes from specific group meetings. Thus access needs to be limited to protect the confidentiality of individual responses.

On the other hand, the question of how wide access should be, given the possibly controversial nature of some of the data, needs to be considered. Managers, who may subscribe to the general principle of data sharing, frequently become defensive and resistant to openly sharing data when the data are critical of management or of certain individuals or groups in the organization. Thus a general tendency is to be overprotective of data and to restrict data access to those in management (or those in control of the data collection-feedback activities). Again safeguards should be built into the contract to ensure that all of those involved will be able to see the data in a specified form.

Timing is another element that should be included in the contract. By specifying goals, a coordination structure, and plans for collection, access, and use, previous contract items have implied that a series of events will occur. It is important to specify the time periods over which these events will occur in order to prevent unrealistic expectations from being created (e.g., interview data will be ready for feedback two days after interviews are finished) or in order to prevent time factors from being used for defensive purposes (e.g., everyone will be able to see the data . . . sometime within the next year).

The success or failure of the project is an issue that often receives much attention at the end of a specified time period in a project, but little attention during the early stages. For effective evaluation plans must be made *before* not *after* work has begun. Again, while details can be worked out with the client after the contract has been put together, some agreement should be reached on whether the project activities will be evaluated, in what way, and by whom.

The contract should specify the resources that the consultant and the organization will provide. It should include the amount of time the consultant will provide, the tasks he or she will perform, and the products he or she will produce. It should also include such things as the consultant's fee, the logistical support (computer time, etc.), the indirect support (release time for employees for group meetings, etc.), and the policy support (i.e., that managers should be attending training sessions on using feedback, etc.) to be provided by the organization.

Finally, the contract should include a procedure for reviewing the relationship, should either party feel this necessary. It should specify how either party can legitimately raise the issue of whether the relationship is progressing as expected and whether changes are needed.

From this discussion, one might get the impression that a contract is only a piece of paper; it is much more than that. Contracting is a process through which the client and consultant share expectations and reach agreement about the basic structure of their relationship. Decisions made during a contracting affect the relationship that is to exist over a period of months or years. It is therefore a very significant event in the life of a change effort. For this reason, contracting may take a considerable amount of time.

For a contract to work, both sides need to understand what is involved. Many consultants spend considerable time educating their clients through discussions, proposals, and presentations on the nature of the process that the client is committing to. This is also part of the contracting process and should precede the final "go" decision, indicated by the client's signing of a contract or letter of agreement. The goal of a contract and/or a contracting process is to help the client to understand what the change activity is about and its implications for organizational, group, and individual functioning. Thus the client can make a free and informed commitment to the process—a commitment that will help to make the data-collection and feedback activity useful and constructive.

PLANNING WHAT DATA TO COLLECT

Once a contract has been developed and the client and consultant have given the "go-ahead" signal on a relationship, the planning process should continue at a more detailed level. Specific decisions need to be made about what data to collect, how to collect it, how to use it, and how to evaluate the entire project. Collection issues will be considered first.

There are many types of information that can be collected in an organization. The possible range and volume of data that might be used for diagnostic and intervention purposes is staggering. No one attempt to collect data could possibly gather all the information that might be relevant to the health of an organization. Some data will be collected and some data will be ignored. The choice of which data to collect and which data to ignore is a critical one, one which will shape the events that follow.

Data collection can also be expensive. Depending upon the method of collection used, a great deal of time can be spent by organizational members in data collection. Collection can be costly in the way that it generates and directs energy. Collecting irrelevant or trivial data not only wastes resources but it also sends a message to people in the organization that the change agent may not know what's going on. Such a message can lead people to doubt the ability of the change agent to help them. Conversely, if data collection is aimed at relevant and important issues in the organization and done in a way that conveys concern for confidentiality, the collection may arouse interest and build motivation among people to work with the data once fed back. Depending on how the collection is performed, the energy generated can be beneficial or harmful.

It is therefore important to decide in advance what kind of data to collect and how to collect it. What will be argued here is that *effective, useful and economical data collection requires a knowledge of organizations (in general), combined with a knowledge of the client organization (specifically).* In addition, a knowledge of the technology of data collection is also needed. (This will be discussed in the following chapters.) Planning for data collection thus needs to be done in a way so that this knowledge, both general and specific, can be employed.

A general knowledge of organizations is important in guiding data collection and in helping to make some very basic decisions about what data to collect to and what data to ignore. There are obviously similarities in the nature of organizational behavior and functioning which cut across the many different types of organizations, and there is a body of knowledge which can help to deal with the basic issue of "what to look at" in an organization. At the same time, each organization has factors that are unique to it. The people in an organization, the organization's technology, the work it performs, etc. create a culture unique to the organization. It has its own language and coding schemes, symbols, and problems which may include issues that are unique to that situation. An understanding of the particular organizational setting and culture is also needed to guide collection and to aid in asking questions in a meaningful manner as well as interpreting responses.

Some questions which should be asked *prior* to the collection of data are: What data should be collected? From what sources can the data be obtained? How should the data be collected? The consultant should be concerned with how to obtain the answers to these questions

in a way that will enable the application of general and specific knowledge. Four sources are particularly helpful in obtaining information
about data collection: general models of organizational functioning,
preliminary data collection, the specific knowledge of organizational
members, and the technical knowledge of the consultant. (See Fig.
5.1.) One source is general models of organization. A consultant
should enter a situation with a general picture or map of how organizations function and why people behave as they do in organizational
settings. These models help the consultant to decide what to pay attention to as well as how to put pieces of data together to obtain a coherent picture of how the organization works, what seems to be working
well, and what seems to be working poorly.

Many different organization models exist and are frequently used
by change agents. For example, Lawrence and Lorsch (1969) describe
a model they use for diagnosis and change; it focuses on the interfaces
between individuals, the organization, and the environment. Galbraith's (1973) model is another example; it concentrates on questions
of organizational structure and design by examining the amount of
uncertainty the organization faces. A very broad organizational
model has also been outlined by Nadler and Tushman (1977); it

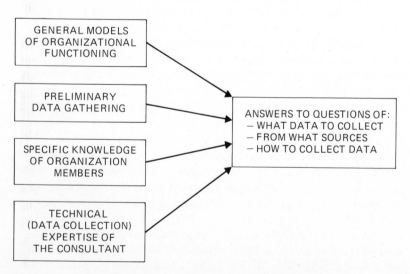

Fig. 5.1 Sources of guidance on data collection.

focuses on the consistency between the major organizational components of tasks, individuals, formal organizational arrangements, and
the informal organization. Such models are useful because they guide
the change agent in his or her search for data. This can be seen in one
approach to survey feedback (Bowers and Franklin, 1975) which is
based on Likert's (1961, 1967) model of organizational functioning.
The questionnaire instrument used in this approach (Taylor and
Bowers, 1972) focuses heavily on issues of leadership, group processes, organizational climate, and satisfaction, since these are the
major variables in the model.

Having a valid, effective and tested model therefore guides the
consultant to certain types of information and sources. Many people
carry models "in their heads" which guide their observations and data
collection, but they are often not aware of those models or how the
models direct or limit the information collected. It is therefore important for the consultant to be aware of his or her own model (or
models) and to constantly ask the question "Is my model applicable in
this situation?" One way of testing whether the model is applicable is
to share the model with the members of the organization so that they
can determine whether the model is useful or not.

The initial investigations, observations, and tentative data collection done by the consultant during the scouting and entry phase is a
second source of knowledge regarding what data to collect. In PNB,
for example, before the consultants started the process of determining
what data would be collected by the feedback system, they conducted
some initial investigatory work in the 20 branches of the bank. Their
particular approach to working with organizations involved briefing
all organizational members *before* the project started. All of the
branch managers were given a short presentation about the project
and were also given the opportunity to discuss it and ask questions.
Similar meetings were held with assistant managers and teller supervisors. Following these meetings, a brief meeting was held by the consultants with the staff at each of the 20 branches. These meetings were
followed by relatively short (30-minute) open-ended interviews with
the manager, assistant manager, and teller supervisor in each branch,
conducted by the consultants, who were also given a tour of the
branch. The consultants then spent about two hours observing branch
activities (sitting next to a teller or a loan officer and talking with them
as they did their work).

The consultants then began to assemble the data, (which included observations and interviews) to obtain a tentative picture of the branch system and a profile of differences and similarities among the branches. This gave the consultants a basic understanding of the organization before they began planning for the structured data collection that would be a part of the feedback system. Thus the consultants began the process of designing a feedback system with some knowledge of the basic business (banking) and its technology, an awareness of the language and coding schemes used (for example, "cracking off," "over and short," "CD's," "delinquency," etc.), and some initial perceptions of the problems individuals faced at the branches.

A third source of knowledge about what information to collect is the people in the organization. The organization's members obviously have a great deal of knowledge about how the system works. While the employees' organization models are probably less complete than the consultant's, these individuals do have valuable information about how the system works, what kinds of problems (or at least the symptoms of the problems) exist, and where different information can be found. One of the best ways of using this knowledge is to actively involve organizational members in the planning for the data-collection/feedback cycle *and* data collection specifically. As the planning for data collection proceeds, organizational members can work with the consultant; help to interpret initial data collection; test the applicability of general models; direct the consultant to areas of perceived problems and data sources; and help him or her identify valid data.

Again, the PNB case provides a useful illustration. The cross-sectional task force played an important role in deciding what data would be included in the feedback system. The academic models, though useful, could not provide the answers to the critical questions, "What kinds of data do people who work in bank branches want to receive?" and "What kinds of data will be useful?" The task-force representatives could best answer those questions.

The consultant, a fourth source of knowledge, may also have relevant information about the technology of data collection. The consultant, together with his internal partners, can determine some of the general strategies for data collection. Some decisions should be made jointly such as deciding whether to use interviews, observations, or questionnaires, etc. In certain instances, however, the consultant may have a particular expertise (which he or she may ultimately want to transfer to his or her internal partners). The consultant may be knowledgeable about the technical aspects of information collection, such as interviewing methods, observation schemes, questionnaire construction, data analysis, etc. In the PNB case, the consultants were helpful in creating the short-form questionnaire. Once the task force decided on the questions to be asked, the consultants helped with the specific wording of the questions and the formatting of responses.

The ideal situation, of course, is one where the four types of knowledge are combined and used to design the data-collection strategy and activities. This situation argues for a collaborative process between the change agent and his or her internal partners, since that approach permits the relatively easy combination of the different viewpoints. It also becomes clear that consultants should have useful and valid models of organizational functioning *before* they enter an organization. They also need to do initial scouting and data collection in order to get oriented to the specific issues, language, and culture of the client organization. Change agents should select internal partners to work with them on designing data collection methods. They should also have a knowledge of and a willingness to use different types of data collection technologies as appropriate.

PLANNING HOW TO USE DATA

The theory of information and behavior states that *how* data are used is a critical factor in determining the kind of energy generated by the feedback process. The detailed concerns of how to use data—the stages of analysis, feedback, and follow-up—will be discussed in the chapters that follow. It is important to note here, however, that the process of data use (i.e., analysis, feedback, and follow-up) also needs to be planned for in advance. Organization members want and need information about how the data they are giving to the consultants will be used. In the absence of such information, people frequently create fantasies about how the data will be used. (For example, "everyone who indicates dissatisfaction will be fired," or "if we say that we are satisfied with our pay, we won't get a pay raise this year."). These fantasies create expectations which in turn lead to behavior that may be harmful to the larger change effort.

Thus early in the data-collection/feedback cycle the consultant and his or her internal partners need to develop a clear plan for using the data that they collect—a plan that will be clearly understood by all participating members of the organization. Again, a number of questions have to be answered.

First, questions of analysis must be answered. What type of investigations will be done with the data, how can the data be used in the most helpful way, and who will do the actual analysis? Second, there are questions concerning data feedback, such as how much data will be fed back and in what form (raw or processed, detailed or summarized, etc.). Third, there are questions about the order in which data will be presented to organization members. Will top management see the data first, will lower level employees see it first, or will a labor-management committee see it first? Fourth, there are questions concerning data feedback and use. Will the data be presented at meetings or in written reports? Who will run the meetings? How many meetings will there be? What will the meetings be like, etc.? Finally, there are questions of resources and commitments (from individuals, management, or labor). What is needed to make the process that is developed work?

In answering these questions (as with the questions of data collection), relevant knowledge can be obtained from both the organization and the consultant. The consultant should bring a range of models of analysis and feedback that are available. (See Chapter 8 for discussions of various models.) Ideally the consultant should have available several different models, with different strengths and weaknesses and different degrees of applicability in different types of organizations (or where there are different kinds of problems). Internal partners should also have some idea of which strategies and procedures for using the data will work in this particular organization, as well as what kinds of resources are necessary to make them work well. Again, the kinds of information needed point to a collaborative process between the consultant and a group that represents the interests of various subgroups within the organization.

The implication is that the consultant needs to have several models that will bring about the kind of data usage which will create and direct energy towards problem solving and improved ways of working together. The consultant needs to be flexible in the application of the models and open to the possibility of constructing new "hybrid" models as he or she combines his or her knowledge with that of internal partners to build a useful approach. Finally, all of this preparation should be done *before*, not *after*, data collection.

PLANNING EVALUATION

One area frequently overlooked in the planning stage is evaluation, an important part of any change effort. Both consultants and organizational members make their own evaluations of change, but they frequently base their evaluations on incomplete success criteria and limited or very subjective data. Systematic evaluation is useful for a number of very practical reasons. Without systematic evaluation it is often hard to determine what the effects of the intervention activity were. Organizational members may appear to feel better, but this should not be the only criterion for evaluating whether the resources, time, and effort put into the change activity were worth it, to either the individuals or the organization.

Evaluation can be valuable in helping the consultant and the organization to learn from their work—that is, to learn what has gone well or what has gone poorly and why, to learn about themselves, and to learn about what changes would be desirable or possible. Evaluation is also important if the case for continuation or diffusion of change is to be made. Individuals and the organization should make their own cost-benefit analyses concerning how much the change activities cost and the benefits received from them. Based on these analyses, they can make decisions about the future and, if needed, make a case for the continuation or termination of the project, based on some objective data. All of these factors therefore indicate a need for planned and systematic evaluation of data-based activities.

Evaluation is frequently seen as something that is done *after* a period of change activity has passed. At that point, the organization and the change agent may attempt to determine whether the work to date has been successful or not. This is what usually happens; however, there are several reasons why evaluation, like planning for data collection and use, should be done early, ideally before the major data-collection activity begins. One specific reason why evaluation should be done early in the project is because as the program unfolds, people may begin to have different reactions to it (favorable or unfavorable), and therefore may have differing interests in either seeing the program succeed and continue or seeing the program fail and be terminated. Individuals or groups may pick criteria for evaluation, after the fact, that will support their position on the change activity. Objective evaluation thus requires the identification of criteria and the noting of bench marks for the measurement of change, *before* the work begins. Secondly, the mechanics of evaluation require that attention be given to it early in the cycle. For example, evaluation may require "before" and "after" measures on certain types of information (i.e. absenteeism, productivity, employee accidents, mental health, attitudes, etc.). Frequently it is impossible to get the "before" data at the end of a period of change activity. Planning should be done for it before it is needed.

Evaluation can be a painful and anxiety-producing process. It is often difficult for a consultant or an organization to look critically at what has been accomplished together, particularly if they suspect failure. For that reason, evaluation frequently is not done at all. Again, the need to plan for evaluation (to ensure that it will occur) is clear.

In the planning process, a number of questions must be answered in order to build in evaluation. First, consideration should be given to the criteria or bench marks to be used. How do we determine whether things have gone well or not? Again, the Winfield case gives us an example of this. The consultant and the client jointly identified several areas that would be indicators of the success or failure of the change program. Implicit in determining criteria is determining how the criteria will be measured and what data may need to be collected for evaluation (as opposed to diagnosis or intervention) purposes. Second, timing questions are important. When should the evaluation (or evaluations) be conducted? When will be the appropriate time for the consultant and client to stop and take a look at how they are doing? Third is the question of what kind of design changes will need to be made, specifically, what alterations will need to be made in the way in which change activity is implemented in order to facilitate evaluation. An example is found in the PNB case where management agreed to implement the feedback system initially in only 10 of its 20 branches so that the consultants would have a control group against which to compare the changes in the 10 experimental branches. Finally, there is the question of who will do the evaluation, which includes issues of who will supervise it, who will see the results, and who will decide how evaluation results will be acted on.

Again, the approach of working with a representative group within the organization is extremely useful. The consultant may have certain technical expertise on evaluation, but the organization's members have a knowledge of which criteria are really meaningful, which sources of data are valid, and which criteria are important with regard to the organization and the individuals in it. This again argues for a collaborative process for planning, implementing, and making use of evaluation.

6
THE PROCESS OF COLLECTING DATA

Data are collected to obtain valid information about the organization. The effort and expense of collecting data in an organization is worthwhile because the information that is obtained is valuable for diagnosis, for analysis, and for feedback. Data collection, however, can and should be much more. For instance, data collection activities frequently provide the members of an organization with their first in-depth contact with a change agent. First impressions that are formed during the data-collection process may color the entire relationship. Similarly, data collection by itself may be an intervention; it may arouse interest, create energy, or attract attention. Finally, data collection is an integral part of the collection-feedback cycle. It is an important activity that builds toward feedback.

Given that data collection can serve a number of different purposes, three specific questions need to be considered when thinking about gathering data in organizations. First is the question of the goals of data collection. What is the change agent trying to achieve during the period of collection? The answer is important since the nature of these goals may affect the choices that are made about how data will be collected. Once the goals of data collection have been identified, a second question arises. What kind of process should be used for data collection in order to meet those goals? Third is the question of technique. What methods or tools for data collection are available and what advantages or disadvantages does each method have? In this chapter we will examine the first two questions of the goals and the process of data collection, leaving the question of techniques to be answered in the following chapter.

GOALS OF DATA COLLECTION

Valid Information

The most *immediate* goal of data collection is, of course, to obtain information about organizational functioning, effectiveness, and health. From a variety of sources (including the perceptions of organizational members; the behavior of individuals and groups as observed; and the records of organizational performance), data collection is undertaken to enable the change agent and his or her internal partners to compose a picture of how the organization runs, what seems to be going well, and what appear to be major problems. If data are to be used for creating such a picture, a basic requirement is that the data be valid. In simple terms, the data should reflect how the organization actually functions. To be valid, the information should be accurate, reliable, and complete. Ideally, different types of information will be collected from multiple sources and used to assemble a picture of organizational functioning.

Creation and Direction of Energy

Beyond the goal of obtaining information, data collection activities can have other goals and perform other functions. The theory and research on information and behavior imply that collection activities can both generate and direct the energies of organizational members. Thus the change agent can use the data-collection process to begin to build energy that is directed toward using feedback data and creating constructive change in the organization.

Data collection can serve a number of functions in this area. Collection can be used for consciousness raising—getting people thinking about issues concerning them and the organization. For example, by asking questions (on a questionnaire or in an interview), the change agent begins to focus employees' attention on important questions or problems in the organization. In addition, the collection activity itself can create expectations that change is possible and that change may indeed occur in the future. The simple act of asking employees for their opinions and perceptions sends a message that someone in the organization cares about what employees think. This message can raise expectations and create energy. People begin to feel that something is going to happen and that something will be done about critical problems.

It is clear that data collection in and of itself is an intervention into organizational life. By entering into the life of an organization and collecting data from and about the people in that organization, the change agent is intervening. Obviously, collection as an intervention has risks as well as potential benefits. A major risk is raising expectations that cannot be met. This was seen in the Northeastern Hospital case. The consultants, through their extensive and thorough data collection, created the impression that major changes would occur in the hospital once the diagnosis was completed. As the report date drew near, people in the hospital began to get excited and to look forward to some major changes and improvements in the organization. When the project failed to bring about changes, many of the people in the organization became deeply depressed and even more dissatisfied than they had previously been. The act of data collection had raised expectations that could not be met within the constraints of that project. When those expectations were not met, people became dissatisfied and upset.

Relationship Building

Data-collection activities can be used to continue the process of relationship-building between the change agent, his or her internal partners, and the organization. During the planning stage, much work is done on building a relationship between the change agent and a group of people within the organization with which he or she will work closely. While the data is being collected, however, is usually the time when most organization members will have their first chance to see the change agent in action. Many organization members may have had limited contact with the project or the consultant (through presentations, memos, or initial meetings). The collection activities therefore provide a chance to see the consultant in action, to see what he or she is interested in, and to get a more substantial picture of who this person is and what he or she is trying to do. The data collection activities give this information in several ways. The consultant, through his or her selection of what data to collect, sends out a message about his or her goals. If the consultant is concerned with efficiency data, for example, but not with the feelings of individuals, a message about his or her priorities is transmitted. The consultant also gives out information about him or herself through the processes that are used to collect data. To the extent that the consultant works exclusively with management in preparing, planning, and implementing data collection as opposed to working with groups of employees, a message is transmitted concerning how future change activities may be conducted. Finally, the consultant through the nature of face-to-face interactions with people during data collection provides information about what kind of person he or she is, whether he or she understands what it's like to work in this organization, and whether he or she can be trusted. Data collection therefore provides an opportunity for the consultant. If the consultant is able to convey a message to people in the organization that he or she is a person they can trust, is anxious to work with them, and has the potential for helping to improve the organization, he or she may be able to use data collection to build a relationship of trust and openness that can continue through the subsequent change activities.

Frequently the opportunity for relationship-building through data collection is not well used. For example, in the case involving the manager of an industrial products division, a situation where the consultant made little effort to use data collection as a way of building a relationship with people in the organization was described. Questionnaires were sent to employees by mail; the only explanation was a letter from management. Similarly the questionnaires were returned by mail. The employees never saw the consultant, never knew how the questionnaire data might be used, and never had a chance to ask questions or express any concerns that might be raised by a questionnaire of this sort. The collection was done in an impersonal manner, giving the respondents relatively little information and therefore little reason to complete and return the survey. It is not surprising therefore that only about half of the questionnaires were returned.

What this case underscores is that the goals of data-collection can only be achieved by giving careful attention to the process of collecting data—that is, how the data-collection activities are to be carried out.

THE PROCESS OF COLLECTING DATA

A team of consultants working in a large organization decided to administer a questionnaire to obtain data for diagnosis and feedback. Different team members went to different departments and held meetings at which the questionnaire was administered. When the questionnaires were collected, it became clear that the response rate from different departments varied widely, with almost a 100 percent response in some departments and under a 50 percent response in others. This seemed strange. The project was organization-wide; the same questionnaire was used in each case; and there seemed to be no pattern of differences between the high-response and low-response departments. Only later was it discovered that all of the low-responding departments were those in which the questionnaire was administered by one particular team member. Something in the way that team member had presented himself, the project, and the questionnaire had resulted in a lower level of motivation by the respondents to return their questionnaires.

This example again illustrates how the process of collecting data (whether by interview, questionnaire, observation, or examination of organizational records) can affect the quality of the data obtained. (See Williams, Seyboldt, and Pinder, 1975.) It is important to examine what can be done to aid in the collection of valid data, the building of rapport, and the generation of energy.

In general, people in organizations like to provide information because it makes them feel that their observations and feelings are valuable and that others value them also. Individuals are motivated to communicate their concerns by the hope that this information will result in positive change in the organization. On the other hand, there can be a great deal of discomfort surrounding data collection. Many people may fear what will be done with the data they provide, particularly if that information is critical or threatening. They may also experience anxiety concerning the collection activities. The questionnaires may remind them of tests or examinations and the observations may cause them to feel uncomfortable. (Who wants someone watching their every move as they work?) In addition, a general distrust of management and/or outsiders may contribute to the anxiety that employees experience during data collection.

Obviously, the consultant and his or her internal partners need to address these concerns if data-collection activities are to meet their goals. One way of ensuring that the data-collection process will be effective is to emphasize contract building between the data collectors (consultants) and those who are to provide the data within the organization (respondents).

Building a Data-collection Contract

Although a contract between the consultant and the organization may exist, it is important, (for many of the same reasons mentioned in the previous chapter) to build another contract directly between the consultant and the respondents. In some cases, this can be done by distributing a copy of the basic contract previously developed between the consultant and the organization. In most situations, however, it is useful for the consultant to spend time talking with groups of people from whom information will be collected. The purpose is to provide the respondents with a clear picture of what the consultant is like, why the data are being collected, and what the data collection will involve. Frequently this may call for a pre-data collection presentation. In the Northeastern Hospital example, each shift on each nursing unit had a short meeting with one member of the consulting team to discuss the project before any data collection began. In one sense, the team built 19 different contracts with the 19 nursing units before they started their work. In other situations, a brief presentation before the first data collection (be it interview, questionnaire, or observation) may suffice.

The data collection contract may be similar in many ways to the general contract that is negotiated by the consultant and the organization. The collection contract is meant to clarify expectations and define the conditions for a relationship, much as the general contract is meant to do. One difference is the immediacy of the collection contract. The primary concern of the consultant, upon entering a situation to collect data, must be to alleviate some of the anxiety that normally arises during data collection so that valid data can be collected and positive energy can be created. Therefore, one way of structuring the contract is to think about the questions that people in the organization might pose to the consultant when confronted with a request to

Table 6.1

The data collection contract.

(Questions to be resolved between the change agent
and those from whom he or she is collecting data.)

1. Who am I?
2. Why am I here and what am I doing?
3. Who do I work for?
4. What do I want from you and why?
5. How will I protect the confidentiality of your responses?
6. Who will have access to the data?
7. What's in it for you?
8. Can I be trusted?

collect data. The answers given to these questions can be used as one
format for the contracting discussion (see Table 6.1):

1. *Who Am I?*   The first question which the consultant needs to respond to concerns who he or she is. At the start, the consultant is a
stranger or outsider. In the absence of other information, the consultant may be perceived as an extension of management. The consultant
may also be identified with other consultants who may have come into
the organization in the past (efficiency experts, "labor-relations spe-
cialists," etc.). Thus the consultant needs to identify who he or she is
in some terms that will enable organizational members to begin to
understand what kind of person he or she is and where he or she fits
in.

2. *Why Am I Here and What Am I Doing?*   In the course of identification, the consultant needs to state why he or she is here in this organization at this specific time and place (e.g., for introduction and
data-collection purposes). At this point, some of the written general
contract material may be helpful in defining what the goals of the data
collection and subsequent activities are, as seen by management, the
consultant, and any relevant groups. The consultant needs to identify
the basic goals of the data-based activities as well as his or her immediate task of gathering data from this group of people.

3. *Who Do I Work For?*   As a final step in identifying who the consultant is, some information about who the consultant is working for should be provided. Is the consultant working for management, for a group of people in management, for a group of employees and managers, etc.? If the consultant primarily works with management, but sees the ultimate client as the whole organization, this point should be made and specific examples and illustrations that will make that concept clear should be given.

If a major goal of contracting is to build trust and gain support so that organization members will cooperate with the data collection, it is helpful to involve them in the consultant's work of presentation and contracting. For example, if a consultant is working with the support and approval of management, it may be helpful to have management send out a letter identifying the consultant and describing what he or she will be doing, and urging people to cooperate. One consultant, when first meeting with groups, insists on being introduced by either the supervisor or the manager who is the next level up in the hierarchy. This provides the consultant with credibility as he enters the meeting and it is a concrete indication of management's commitment to work with the consultant to collect and use data constructively.

Where the client is a joint employee-manager group, or a labor-management committee, the collection contract is an ideal time to build on the representative nature of the client. Again, many consultants using this kind of arrangement have themselves introduced to work groups by two individuals, a member of management and an employee representative. The presence of these two individuals illustrates very clearly the collaborative nature of the data-based activities.

4. *What Do I Want From You and Why?*   Once the consultant has been identified in terms of his or her client, task, and personal characteristics, the next question is what does the consultant want from the people that he or she will be meeting with. The consultant needs to lay out in very concrete terms, what he or she is asking of people. First, the consultant is asking for the time and the opportunity to speak with them. Second, the consultant is asking them for the time and effort involved in providing data, by asking respondents to fill out questionnaires, be interviewed, or consent to be observed. Implicit is a request

for the group members to trust the consultant and provide open, honest, and valid data. Third, the consultant is asking them for time and effort to work with the data once it has been collected and analyzed.

When explaining to the respondents what is expected of them, the consultant should think about those people who, for one reason or another, may not feel comfortable in providing data. Some employees may not want to give data for any of a number of reasons, ranging from mistrust of management, to previous experiences with consultants, to issues of personal privacy. One way of coping with this problem is to make clear the voluntary nature of the data-collection activities. While asking for cooperation, the consultant can stress that the individuals will be free to not respond if they so desire. This provides a way for the consultant to respect the rights of individuals who do not want to participate while encouraging others to cooperate.

5. *How Will I Protect Your Confidentiality?*   Once the consultant identifies his or her reason for data collection, a number of questions usually occur to the respondents. Perhaps the most critical question is that of confidentiality. When people in an organization are asked to provide data, particularly data concerning their perceptions and attitudes, one of their major concerns is who will see those data and in what form. While some individuals will claim to answer questions honestly, regardless of who sees the data, others will be concerned about protection of their privacy concerning their attitudes and feelings. Some will be concerned about the possible effects of identification (such as reprisals from supervisors, coworkers, or management), while others are concerned about general issues of privacy. It is therefore crucial to guarantee the confidentiality of individual data responses. The guarantee in itself may not be enough, however. The consultant needs to demonstrate, through his or her methods and how the data are treated, that the confidentiality issue will be taken seriously. For example, to say that responses will be treated in a confidential manner and then to ask people to leave questionnaires with their names on them on a table in the center of a work area for several hours until they are picked up is an apparent contradiction.

The easiest way of assuring confidentiality is to make responses anonymous—no names or identifying data will be indicated on the data-collection forms. This is frequently possible, but in some cases respondents may need to be identified by the consultants—to match questionnaire data with observational data, to compare questionnaires administered at one time with questionnaires administered at another time, to make comparisons between work units or levels of the hierarchy, etc. In these cases, usually involving questionnaire data, it is important to identify the employees in a way that will protect confidentiality and to explain to the respondents both the rationale for identification and the safeguards built into the identification system.

An example of an identification system that provides confidentiality is that used by a consulting group with assigns each employee in the organization an identification number, but keeps the list of names and numbers outside of the client organization. The respondent receives the questionnaire in an envelope with his or her name on it; inside the envelope is the questionnaire with the identification number on a gummed label (but no name) and a blank envelope. The respondent completes the questionnaire, discards the envelope with his or her name on it, and returns the questionnaire in the blank envelope directly to the consultant. Another type of identification system was used for the feedback system in the PNB case, where each person was issued an ID card with an identification number on it by the consultants. This number, which only the consultants and the respondent knew, was put on the feedback questionnaires by the respondents when they filled out the questionnaire and it was used to match up the performance data with the questionnaire data for feedback.

6. *Who Will Have Access to the Data?*   The reverse side of the confidentiality question is the question of access. The respondents will want to know if they will have access to the results of this data collection and if so, in what form. A related question is who else will see these data. The first question reflects a natural curiosity about data collection that develops. Individuals having been asked to provide data, want to see the results. The second question reflects a concern with the ultimate use of the data. Will anyone with the power to make changes see the data and be able to act on it?

7. *What's In It For You?*   Ultimately, the respondents will make a decision to provide valid data or not based on an assessment of the costs and benefits of responding. The costs are determined by the amount of time and effort needed to provide data as well as by the risks that come about from being measured or revealing attitudes and

feelings (the confidentiality issue). The benefits and payoffs are usually unclear. The consultant therefore needs to specify the benefits he or she thinks the respondents will receive from the data-based activities. To do this, the consultant may need to describe in detail the procedures for feedback and ultimate use of the data in order to support any claims that the data will help to improve the organization as a place to work. The consultant needs to convince the respondents that the benefits that may occur as a result of the data collection will outweigh the costs of providing the data.

8. *Can I Be Trusted?* Underlying these questions and the whole process of contracting for data collection is the basic question of whether the consultant can be trusted. If the respondents trust the consultant, they will probably provide honest and open information. If they do not trust the consultant, they may distort information, introduce biases, and prevent access to data. This implies that while the content of the contract is important, the way in which the contract is presented is also critical. In face-to-face interactions with the respondents, the consultant needs to convey an understanding of their anxiety, as well as his or her concern for their very natural questions of confidentiality, access, and payoffs. The consultant needs to convey that he or she takes very seriously the task of collecting and safeguarding the data provided by the respondents. The consultant's statements to and actions with the group need to be consistent with the statements made and actions taken with other groups in the organization.

In most cases, the formulation of a collection contract results from a presentation and discussion of issues between the consultant and the respondents. Unlike the general contract, the collection contract frequently is not written, although it is sometimes useful to post a list of "questions and answers" about the data collection at different locations in the organization. A written document serves as a follow-up for the discussions and is a way of conveying information to employees who may not have attended the meetings where the consultant was introduced.

During the discussion of the contract, it is important to provide respondents with an opportunity to ask questions. This questioning is important because in the course of contracting the consultant may not be able to anticipate all of the concerns and questions that a group of respondents might have. The questioning is also important because it allows the respondents to "test" the consultant to determine whether the consultant is someone they can trust. The group may watch the consultant closely as he or she answers questions, noticing things such as whether the consultant is consistent, answers questions directly, evades questions, is interested in responding to problems, attempts to smooth things over, etc.

The contracting session should consist of a two-way discussion; however, the consultant should probably present a thought-out statement, which outlines the basics of the contract. While such statements may vary depending on circumstances, a general example may be helpful in illustrating some basic points in the contract. The following rough script was used in a recent project where data were being collected. The consultant is meeting with a work group for the first time. He or she is beginning work on an OD project where the client is a joint labor-management committee. Two members of that committee have just introduced the consultant to the work group:

> Good morning. My name is _____
> and I want to spend a few minutes with you this morning talking
> about a project that involves this group, as well as the entire orga-
> nization.
>
> Most of you have probably heard about the "Organizational Im-
> provement Project" that started a few weeks ago. In fact, I spoke
> with some of you not long ago. As you may remember, the Orga-
> nizational Improvement Project is a joint labor-management
> effort that is attempting to find ways of improving this organiza-
> tion. Our goal is to make the organization work more effectively
> while also trying to make it a better place to work. The project is
> run by a committee composed of representatives from labor and
> management. The two people who introduced me are part of that
> committee.
>
> My job involves working with the labor-management committee
> and with you as a consultant or helper. I am a behavioral scientist
> and I spend much of my time working with people in organiza-
> tions in projects such as this one. My task is to help you and the
> committee improve things around here, not to make changes my-
> self.
>
> With that information as background, why am I here today? As a
> first step in the project, we need to get a clear picture of how this
> organization runs. What things run well and what things cause

problems? One of the best ways of answering these questions is to ask you, the people who work here, to share your opinions and ideas with us. So our first step is to be data collection, and we are going to ask you to help us by filling out a questionnaire. Before I discuss the questionnaire, are there any general questions about the project, who I am, or things like that?

As I said, the first step in our data collection will involve a questionnaire. In a few minutes I am going to distribute copies of a survey that we are going to ask each of you to fill out. This survey was constructed by the labor-management committee and includes a number of questions that have been asked before in many different organizations, as well as a number of specific questions that were written by the committee especially for this organization.

Although each of you will be asked to help us by filling out a questionnaire, your participation is completely voluntary. If there are any questions that you would rather not answer, please feel free to leave them blank. If you feel you'd rather not fill out the questionnaire at all, that's OK too. No one in this organization will know whether or not you have completed a questionnaire and, in fact, there is no way for me to know who has handed back a questionnaire and who hasn't.

Of course, for this project to work, we need your cooperation and in particular your views, opinions, and attitudes. We'd like to know how you see things around here as openly and honestly as possible. Therefore, we're asking for your help.

A natural question that you might have is, "Who's going to see my questionnaire once it is filled out?" This brings up the question of confidentiality. There is no place on the questionnaire for you to put your name. All responses will be completely anonymous. When you complete the questionnaire, we'd like you to seal it in the attached envelope and drop it into one of the locked "drop boxes" that are located in different parts of the plant. I will personally pick up the questionnaires from these boxes and send them to a keypuncher so that your responses can be put on computer cards. I will then destroy the original questionnaires and will be doing all of the analysis of the data on the computer.

There is no way, therefore, that anyone in this organization can ever find out how any one individual responded on the questionnaire. (Stop again for questions.)

Of course, the purpose of this data collection is to obtain information that can be used. I will be preparing summaries of these data. Some of these summaries will be used by the labor-management committee while other data summaries will be provided to you (this group) to use. I will also work with you as you look through the data. All of the data that you will see will be the combined scores for groups. No individual scores will be seen. (Stop for questions.)

Our goals are to use the questionnaires to gather information that will identify problems and to work on solving the problems. We hope that between the work of the labor-management committee and the work that you will be doing with the data, we will be able to make some significant improvements in this organization.

I appreciate your interest. I will hand out the questionnaires in a moment. If you have any questions about the questionnaire or the project, please contact me. I have an office in the plant (give number and phone extension) and I will be around to visit with you periodically.

SUMMARY

Data collection is not a neutral or benign act. It is an intervention into organizational life and therefore needs to be planned for and conducted carefully. If done well, data collection can yield valid information while helping to build energy toward the feedback activities. If done poorly, data collection can create mistrust and suspicion and yield worthless data. The critical task is contracting. The consultant needs to identify who he or she is, create expectations that the data-collection effort will yield payoffs, and finally build a bond of trust between him or herself and the respondents.

7
TECHNIQUES FOR DATA COLLECTION AND ANALYSIS

Data-based methods are essentially tools which change agents or managers can use to learn about and improve organizations. At the heart of the data-collection/feedback cycle is the feedback activity. At the same time, however, the other stages of planning, collection, and analysis are also important because they build toward feedback. So far we have focused on questions relating to the processes of planning and data collection. While process issues are important, so are the more concrete questions of methods and techniques. In order to use data-based methods, the change agent needs to know something about how data can be collected as well as what to do with the data once it is in hand.

This chapter is aimed at exploring a number of the basic techniques and methods for data collection. A few words will also be said about data analysis. (For a discussion of some elementary techniques of data analysis, see Appendix A.) While the purpose of this book and the space available do not allow for a detailed technical discussion, this chapter will at least orient one to the different range of techniques available for collecting data. (For a detailed discussion of these areas, see Babbie, 1972; Bouchard, 1976.)

There are different ways of collecting data on how organizations function and how the people in them feel and behave. There are numerous specific techniques, but most of these fall into one of four broad catagories—that is, interviews, questionnaires, observations, and a final category of secondary data and unobtrusive measures. (See Table 7.1 for a brief comparison of these methods.)

Table 7.1
A comparison of different methods of data collection.

Method	Major advantages	Major potential problems
Interviews	1. Adaptive—allows data collection on a range of possible subjects 2. Source of "rich" data 3. Empathic 4. Process of interviewing can build rapport	1. Can be expensive 2. Interviewer can bias responses 3. Coding/interpretation problems 4. Self-report bias
Questionnaires	1. Responses can be quantified and easily summarized 2. Easy to use with large samples 3. Relatively inexpensive 4. Can obtain large volume of data	1. Nonempathic 2. Predetermined questions may miss issues 3. Data may be over-interpreted 4. Response bias
Observations	1. Collects data on behavior rather than reports of behavior 2. Real-time, not retrospective 3. Adaptive	1. Interpretation and coding problems 2. Sampling is a problem 3. Observer bias/reliability 4. Costly
Secondary data/ unobtrusive measures	1. Nonreactive—no-response bias 2. High face validity 3. Easily quantified	1. Access/retrieval possibly a problem 2. Potential validity problems 3. Coding/interpretation

INTERVIEWS

One of the most obvious, direct, and sensible ways of discovering how an organization functions is to ask the people in it. The members of an organization are valuable sources of data on how the organization functions and how they feel. Organization members can provide a wide range of information. As informants, they can provide the consultant with information about how things work; they are descriptors of the organizational system. Members also have judgments about what things are performing well and what things are performing poorly. If asked, they also are able to reveal the data that they have collected which led to these judgments. Members also have affective reactions to what goes on around them—positive or negative reactions such as feeling happy or dissatisfied, frustrated or complacent, etc. The people in the organization are therefore valuable sources of descriptive information, diagnostic evaluations, and affective reactions.

Most people in organizations, under relatively normal conditions, are ready (and sometimes even anxious) to share their perceptions, evaluations, and feelings. A consultant can thus obtain a large amount of information from the people in an organization by simply asking them questions—that is, by interviewing.

Types of Interviews

Interviews can be conducted in many different ways. (For a comprehensive discussion of interviewing, see Kahn and Cannell, 1967.) Interviews differ in their degree of structure. One type of interview is the *unstructured* interview, where the interviewer provides very little guidance to the respondent in terms of questions or possible answers. In this form of nondirective or client-centered interviewing, the interviewer is only interested in information which the respondent feels is important, and the interviewer attempts to provide only minimal guidance through stimulating discussion and getting the respondent to explore his or her feelings and perceptions in the areas that he or she chooses to. One consultant, who uses unstructured interviews, frequently begins his interviews with the following: "Tell me about this place. How did things get to be the way they are?" Starting with this general question, the consultant continues the interview by clarifying or summarizing what the respondent says, probing occasionally with questions. The interview thus can move in any number of directions.

Another type of interview is the *structured, open-ended* interview. In this case, the interviewer has predetermined questions covering certain topics, but the respondent is unconstrained in his answering. The interviewer may ask a question such as "How do you know when you are performing well or poorly?" and then attempt to write down in as much detail as possible the respondent's answer to the question.

The most structured form of interview is the *structured, fixed-response* interview. Here the interviewer not only provides the questions, but also provides a set of predetermined alternative responses. An example would be the following question.

Which one of the following statements best describes how you feel about your job:

☐ Very satisfied

☐ Satisfied

☐ Neither satisfied nor dissatisfied

☐ Dissatisfied

☐ Very dissatisfied

Frequently this kind of question would be accompanied by a set of response cards, each card having one of the five responses written on it, enabling the respondent to pick the response which is most appropriate. This kind of interview is in many ways an orally administered questionnaire, but it permits options. For example, when an extremely negative or positive response occurs, the interviewer can ask "Why do you feel that way?"

Interviews may vary in ways other than in structure. An interview may be formal (held in a predetermined setting for a set amount of time) or informal (questions are asked while activities are performed, such as during observation of working behavior). Interviews may be conducted individually, or they may be conducted in groups (the people in the group give answers, discuss answers, and react to the answers that others give). Interviews may also vary in their sampling. Everyone in an organization may be interviewed or a subsample may be interviewed. A critical difference here is cost. Formal interviews, individual interviews, and full-sampling interviews cost the organization or the consultant more time and money. On the other hand, different types of interviews yield different kinds of data. Some people may prefer to talk in their natural work setting rather than in a formal away from the job interview, while others prefer to leave their work place for what may be a more private setting. Similarly a group interview may inhibit some people, while stimulating others to talk. Thus the choice of which type of interview to select depends on an assessment of costs as well as an evaluation of the data gathering potential of each method in the particular situation.

An example of a structured, open-ended interview is the short orientation interview (see Appendix B). This interview is used during the early stages of a project to orient the consultant to the basic issues and problems of the organization, before he or she attempts a more systematic or comprehensive data collection. The interview also includes a number of probe questions that are designed to further explore an issue if necessary.

Advantages and Disadvantages of Interviews

Interviews have the major advantage of being adaptive. As the interviewer proceeds with the interview, he or she can modify the questions, choose an area to probe, or make other changes to adapt the interview to the situation. Thus the interview allows collection on a wide range of possible subjects, with the interviewer having the ability to change the interview to emphasize those subjects about which the respondent seems to have information. Open-ended interviews are a potentially rich source of data. The responses may contain detailed information about causes of problems as well as the symptoms. The respondent can explain *why* he or she is satisfied or dissatisfied, as opposed to just indicating *how* satisfied or dissatisfied he or she is, for example. Specific quotations or examples from interviews are often particularly useful during feedback to illustrate a finding or a pattern in the data.

As a collection device, an interview conducted by a good interviewer can be an empathic device. By communicating to the respondent that he or she understands the organization and the problems of being in the organization, the interviewer can communicate empathy with the respondent—an understanding of the respondent and his or her environment. Empathy can very frequently result in the respondent being more willing to open up and disclose possibly threatening information to the interviewer. (Alderfer and Brown, 1972, demonstrated this with questionnaires.) For example, where more empathic methods have been used, respondents seem to be less hesitant about making negative statements about themselves, their coworkers, their supervisors, or their working conditions. Similarly, the whole process of the interview can lead to increased rapport with members of the organization. This rapport can aid both the information collection in the interview itself and the future activities of the change agent in the system. People enjoy talking about their work, and the interview can be a pleasurable and meaningful experience if the respondent feels that the interviewer has listened, understood, and valued what has been said.

Interviews have some potential problems as data collection devices. First, interviews can be expensive. They can consume a great deal of the consultant's time. Second, while the interviewer can elicit responses from the respondent and adapt the interview, the interviewer can also bias the responses with his or her choice of questions to ask and pursue and with the nature of his or her interactions with the respondent, which may encourage or discourage certain responses. Similarly the interviewer's biases may creep into the data that are recorded or omitted. Thus there is the risk of the interview reflecting the biases of the interviewer rather than the perceptions, evaluations, and feelings of the respondent. Open-ended interviews pose a particular problem of coding and interpretation. In order to summarize the findings (either for feedback or analysis) over a number of interviews, some interpretation and category coding of responses is necessary. The process of coding is expensive and provides another possible source of bias (from the coder). Finally there is the basic problem of self-report biases. The interview does not provide direct information on behavior, rather it provides a report on an organization member of behavior and feelings. There are many sources of bias in self-report measures. (See Chapter 2 of Webb *et al.,* 1966, for a listing of sources of error in self-report measures.) The respondent may have biased perceptions, or incomplete information; the respondent may also give the interviewer what he or she thinks the interviewer wants to hear; or the respondent may feel threatened and thus withhold information.

While there are the problems of interviewer, coder, and respondent bias, the interview still remains perhaps the single most-useful data collection tool in an organization. The disadvantages imply that the results of interviews should be validated and used with care, rather than always being accepted at face value.

Using Interviews

In general, interviews are a valuable source of data and should probably be used at some point during the data-collection/feedback cycle. They are particularly useful during the early stages of the relationship when rapport building is important and the consultant is learning about the organization and the people in it. Here the adaptive and flexible nature of the interview is particularly valuable.

An important element in the interviewing method is, of course, the interviewer. Obtaining useful data depends upon having a good interviewer, one who can build rapport, can be empathic, and is aware of (and can control) the interviewer-based biases that might enter the data. Having a skilled interviewer is therefore essential for using this method.

A final concern is that interviewing takes time. Depending upon the number of interviewers and the size of the sample, interviews can take a considerable amount of time to conduct. Once the interview is finished, the process of interpretation and coding can also be lengthy. The turnaround time, therefore, from the beginning of the interviews to the delivery of feedback can be considerable.

The PNB case again provides an illustration. As mentioned, the research team, before putting together any questionnaires, conducted a series of interviews and observations in each of the 20 branches of the bank. As part of their visit to each branch, one of the team members conducted formal interviews of about an hour each with the branch manager, the assistant manager, and the teller supervisor. Informal interviews were conducted with other staff members during the course of observations. The branch manager interview provides an example of the type of questions used. After a brief review of the project, which repeated orientation material presented earlier at a meeting of all branch managers, the manager was asked a number of pre-structured questions, including the following:

How would you describe the branch manager's job?

How do you know when you are doing well and when you are doing poorly on your job?

What kinds of information do you currently receive about your job performance?

What kinds of information do you currently receive about the performance of your branch?

What do you feel are the major problems that face this branch?

Please describe the branch to me. What kinds of people work here? What kinds of jobs do people perform?

Could you describe your own career path? How did you get to be a branch manager?

In all, 15 questions were used to collect some of the basic information about the branch system at PNB. The interviewers attempted to record the managers' answers as exactly as possible. Following the interviews, each member of the research team read all of the interviews and after discussing the interviews, a large chart was constructed with the 20 branches listed on one side and characteristics (such as size, market area, major problems, etc.) on the other. The interview data were used to fill in the chart, providing the researchers with a summary picture of the entire branch system as an organization.

QUESTIONNAIRES

Questionnaires are essentially self-administered interviews. A set of questions are given to the respondent in printed form. The respondent reads the questions and answers, either by writing in an answer or choosing from alternative predetermined responses. As a paper-and-pencil instrument that is not dependent upon a "live" interviewer being present, it allows simultaneous data collection from many people in an organization. With fixed-response questionnaires, quantitative analysis can be done in a short period of time, allowing for a relatively short turnaround time.

The underlying rationale for the questionnaire is similar to the interview. Information is obtained by directly asking the organization members for their perceptions, evaluations, and feelings. The major difference between an interview and a questionnaire is that the questionnaire is self-administered and, as used in organizations, generally tends to make use of fixed responses rather than open-ended responses to questions.

Types of Questionnaires

As with interviews, one of the options available in using a questionnaire is whether the responses are designed to be open-ended or fixed. Because of the problems of coding and a tendency of respondents not to want to write extensive or greatly descriptive answers, most organizational questionnaires are fixed-response. Of the many different types of questions and responses, the one most widely used is the Likert-type item. The respondent is asked to reply to a question or statement by checking a point on a scale of varying degrees of agreement/disagreement, satisfaction, etc. An example of this type of questionnaire item follows:

Below are some statements which describe jobs. How much do you agree or disagree with each statement as a description of your job?

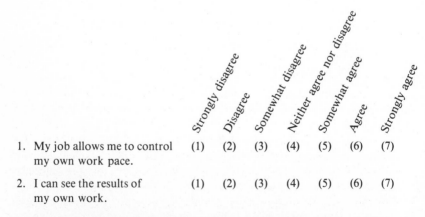

	Strongly disagree	Disagree	Somewhat disagree	Neither agree nor disagree	Somewhat agree	Agree	Strongly agree
1. My job allows me to control my own work pace.	(1)	(2)	(3)	(4)	(5)	(6)	(7)
2. I can see the results of my own work.	(1)	(2)	(3)	(4)	(5)	(6)	(7)

Other questionnaire items may ask the respondent to choose from a number of alternatives, where each alternative has a very specific meaning such as the following:

Which shift do you work on most of the time?

(1) Day shift (7:00 am to 3:00 pm)

(2) Afternoon shift (3:00 pm to 11:00 pm)

(3) Night shift (11:00 pm to 7:00 am)

Questions can also be constructed which ask the respondent to check a number indicating his or her position on a scale described by several descriptive statements, such as the following:

How much *variety* is there in your job?

(1)	(2)	(3)	(4)	(5)	(6)	(7)

Very little: I do pretty much the same things over and over, using the same equipment and procedures almost all the time.

Moderate variety

Very much: I do many things, using a variety of equipment and procedures.

Similarly, the respondent may be asked to check a response on a scale anchored only by two words, as follows:

How do you feel about your present life in general?

Boring	(1)	(2)	(3)	(4)	(5)	(6)	(7)	Interesting
Enjoyable	(1)	(2)	(3)	(4)	(5)	(6)	(7)	Miserable

These examples represent only a few of the many ways in which questions can be constructed, but they illustrate some of the possible alternatives.

Questionnaires can also vary in the scope of their coverage. One might put together a questionnaire that focuses on one particular issue (for example, group process) or one might want to use a questionnaire to get a very broad diagnostic picture of an entire organization.

Another difference in questionnaires is the degree to which they are standardized versus custom-constructed for a situation. Standardized questionnaires have a predetermined set of questions that are designed to be used in almost any situation. These questions have been developed and refined over a period of time, are based on a model of organizational functioning, and have been pretested. The format, responses, and administrative procedures for the questionnaires have also been tested and refined. A large number of standardized questionnaires have been developed and are in use, but they vary greatly in quality. An example of a comprehensive and thoroughly developed instrument can be seen in the *Survey of Organizations* (Taylor and Bowers, 1972), which has been used extensively for diagnostic and survey feedback purposes.

While standardized questionnaires exist, a consultant or a client may want to develop a survey specifically for an organization, adding new questionnaire items that are specific to that situation. A custom-designed survey may better fit the needs of a particular client. This questionnaire might be composed by the consultant, or by the consultant along with his or her internal partners—for example, with a cross-sectional or labor-management group. (For examples of questionnaires, see Appendix B.)

Advantages and Problems of Using Questionnaires

The fixed-response questionnaires have a number of distinct advantages for organizational work. The answers can easily be quantified because the fixed-response questionnaire actually has the respondent doing his at her own coding. The numerical responses can be summarized, aggregated, and subjected to statistical analysis with little or no coding, interpretation, or preparation. Questionnaires can be administered to more than one person at a time and the potentially quick turnaround time makes them easy to use with large samples of people (from several hundred to thousands). Once a questionnaire is developed, the cost of administering it is relatively low. The cost of conducting interviews may be at least three to five times more per respondent than the cost of using questionnaires. Also, with skillful question writing and formatting, a single questionnaire can be used to obtain from an individual a large amount of data on a whole range of topics and issues.

Questionnaires also have drawbacks as data-collection methods. First, questionnaires are nonempathic. A respondent may find it difficult to "warm up" to a questionnaire; it can be a relatively impersonal data-collection process. Questionnaires can be made to be more empathic by using the specific language of the organization, by communicating knowledge of the organization's problems, etc. When this is done, respondents seem more willing to answer questions openly (Alderfer and Brown, 1972). Obviously, a completely standardized questionnaire provides the least empathic form.

Questionnaires by definition are prestructured, self-administered interviews. Since they are prestructured, they are not adaptive. If the questions are not appropriate for a specific respondent, they cannot be changed during the administration. Once the individual has been given the questionnaire, the questions are fixed. Questionnaires may therefore present questions to the respondent to which he or she cannot or will not respond, while disregarding other areas where the respondent may have a rich store of information.

Fixed-response questionnaires present problems in terms of interpretation and analysis. The consultant, his or her internal partners, or whoever does the interpretation and analysis has only the specific checked response alternative to work with on each question. If, for example, a person answered the second sample question on the list given previously ("I can see the results of my work") by checking a [5] response, the analyst does not know why the [5] was checked, what specifically the [5] means, or whether the [5] is a good or bad response. Furthermore, it is not clear whether the [5] means the same thing to this respondent as it might mean to someone else. The data are inherently limited, and their easy quantification can lead one to interpretations that may not be valid.

Finally, questionnaires have in common with interviews the problems of self-report or response biases. Rather than collecting data about behavior itself, the questionnaire collects individuals' reports of behavior, and these reports may be biased (consciously or unconsciously) by the respondent. These biases may include such things as a tendency to answer questions that are next to each other in a similar manner, and a tendency to answer questions later in the questionnaire with less care than earlier questions (a fatigue effect), as well as the other forms of self-report bias mentioned in the discussion of interviews.

Using Questionnaires

Questionnaires are economical and easily used tools for data collection in organizations. The major problem involved in using questionnaires is how to overcome or adjust for the inherent weaknesses of the method so as to capitalize on the strengths of the tool. Several specific concerns need to be considered.

A basic concern is achieving a trade off between the strengths and weaknesses of a standardized questionnaire (reliability, validity, pretested, already constructed, based on a model, nonempathic, nonadaptive) against the strengths and weaknesses of a custom designed questionnaire (not pretested, not model-based, takes time to put together, more empathic, focused toward the particular issues of this organization). Here again, having a group in the organization to work with as an internal partner can be particularly valuable. Such a group can work with the consultant to review different existing instruments and to help make decisions among alternative courses of action. The consultant and the group may, for example, decide that one standardized questionnaire does indeed seem appropriate and thus can be used either "as is" or with minor changes in introductions—for example, putting the name of the organization on the questionnaire and putting appropriate job and organizational titles in the introductions to groups of questions. Another alternative may be that the group finds the standardized questionnaire to be basically good, but additional items may have to be written to tap certain issues or problems that the standardized questionnaire does not cover. Many standardized questionnaires leave space for special questions developed by the specific organization. The group may want to do more than simply add items; in that case, the group may want to adapt a standardized questionnaire for use, deleting the parts of the questionnaire that are not appropriate and adding new items. Another alternative is to put together an original questionnaire, using standardized questionnaires only as sources of pretested and refined questions (or sets of questions). This strategy, of course, depends upon the ownership of the standardized questionnaire and whether or not it is copyrighted. Finally, the consultant and his or her group may decide that the most appropriate questionnaire is one that they collaboratively put together from scratch.

In the various examples given, we saw how different strategies were used. In the hospital case, a standardized questionnaire was used "as is." In the school district case, groups developed their own questionnaires, which were adaptations of a standardized questionnaire. In the bank example, the short feedback questionnaire was developed entirely by the task force in the bank, using standardized questionnaires only as sources of potential individual questions.

In general, working with a group to develop the questionnaire has some major advantages. First, the group can help to identify issues and problems which are unique to the specific organization and which should be addressed by the questionnaire. Second, the group members, having worked on the development of the questionnaire, become expert sources of information for their fellow employees. They now understand what the questionnaire is about, how it will be used, and why certain questions are included. They can respond to questions from other people in the organization in an intelligent and informed manner. Third, the questionnaire is their questionnaire, rather than the consultant's. The process helps to build ownership over the data-based change activities. Finally, the internal partners are important sources of information concerning the culture, symbols, and language of the organization—factors which can greatly affect the usefulness of questionnaire data. Every organization uses different coding schemes or language. A questionnaire which uses inappropriate language or symbols can result in the collection of inaccurate data and can even alienate people. A simple and obvious example can be seen in the section on many questionnaires that asks for information about supervisors. A diagnostic questionnaire should naturally inquire about perceptions and attitudes with regard to supervision. The word "supervisor," however, can mean very different things in different organizations. In the Northeastern Hospital example, a supervisor is a relatively high-level nursing administrator, who has the responsibility for several nursing units and has other levels of supervision (i.e., head nurses, assistant head nurses, charge nurses) reporting to her. In the PNB example, the supervisor is the person who directs the work of the tellers in a branch. The maximum number of people reporting to the supervisor is 11; many people in the branch (i.e., loan officers) have no reporting relationship to the supervisor. In another situation, a consultant was collecting data by questionnaire in a very innovative and participatively structured manufacturing plant. When the questionnaire with the word "supervisor" in it was distributed, it was received with concern and suspicion. The workers in this plant had long ago abondoned the use of the term supervisor and now were working with peer-selected "group leaders." The use of the term "supervisor" in the questionnaire demonstrated a lack of knowledge of and sensitivity to the culture and language of that organization.

Organizations frequently have a history of questionnaire work, and the prior experience may have been positive or negative. Frequently one encounters an organization where questionnaires have been used before with little thought given to their use for systematic and participative change. Thus the consultant may encounter resistance from organization members who say, "We've filled out questionnaires before, but nothing ever happened—management just ignores what we say; they want to make us feel like they're interested in our opinions, but they're not." The consultant should be aware of such history if it exists.

A final problem involves the tendency to "over-questionnaire." Questionnaires are easy to use and it is always easy to add one more question to the survey. Groups working as internal partners frequently fall into the one-more-question trap. The result may be an overly long questionnaire which results in respondent fatigue and resistance, poor quality data, and many questions for which there is no analysis plan because the group "just wanted to see what we'd get" in response to the question.

In summary, questionnaires should obviously be used with careful thought and planning. Together, the questionnaire and the interview can be used to collect a great deal of valuable data. The interview is particularly useful at the beginning of consultant/client relationships, when establishing rapport is important and when the limited amount of information that the consultant has dictates a need for an adaptive data-collection technique. Questionnaires are most useful in collecting data from large numbers of people; their formats lend themselves to easy feedback and permit comparison and evaluation. Thus large-scale systematic data collection in an organization frequently involves some kind of questionnaire. Here too, however, the interview can also be useful in obtaining in-depth data that the questionnaire cannot. Frequently a questionnaire administration is accompanied by an in-depth interview of a small subsample of organization members. The interview data can then be used to test the hypotheses developed from the questionnaire data and to add illustrative detail during feedback.

OBSERVATIONS

One of the most obvious ways of collecting data about behavior in organizations is to observe the behavior as it occurs. Observation is particularly valuable because it removes one possible source of bias, the report of the respondent. It puts the data collector directly in touch with the activities about which data are being collected. Observational methods have been widely used in organizations. Many classic examples of organizational research have relied on the presence of an on-site observer, usually with the data collector as a participant/observer, having an actual role in the organization while systematically watching the behavior that occurred. (See examples and discussions of this method in Whyte, 1955; McCall and Simmons, 1969; or Schatzman and Strauss, 1972.) While also making use of other kinds of data collection, this approach has been based largely on the observation of behavior as it occurs.

A basic question regarding observation is, "How can the observation be structured so that meaningful and useful data can be collected?" There are more things to be observed in an organization than any one consultant or group of consultants can possibly observe and note. Total observation would require large numbers of people being present at all times and in all parts of the organization, and this is usually not feasible. Thus the observations are structured through choices —that is, what to observe and what not to observe; when to observe and when not to observe; what to record and what not to record. Structuring may range from fairly explicit observation guidelines and instruments to frameworks which are not written or specified, but which the consultant uses as a guide while observing behavior in the organization.

The basic strength or weakness of observation as a tool is that the observer is the data-collection instrument (as opposed to the questionnaire or the observation instrument). A sensitive observer making use of an effective structure for observation can be an effective data-collection tool. An observer who has little sensitivity and no guiding structure may spend hours observing, see nothing, and report no usable data.

Types of Observation

Structure is an important factor in observation, and approaches to observation differ in the degree to which they structure both the watching and the recording. One approach, which might be labelled *structured* observation, uses instruments and procedures to direct the observer very specifically to what type of behavior he or she should be observing and to specify exactly how the observations will be recorded. An example of this approach is seen in the Interaction Process Analysis (IPA) framework developed by Bales (1971) for observing and analyzing behavior in small groups. This scheme has the observer noting each interaction between individuals in a group. The observer records who initiated the interaction and to whom it was directed and codes the interaction according to its content, using a standard set of categories.

A second type of observation is the *semi-structured* observation, where observation is only minimally structured, but the recording is specified. An example of this can be seen in the standardized job-observation form (Jenkins, Nadler, Lawler, and Cammann, 1975) used for observing psychological characteristics of jobs. Using this procedure, the observer watches the employee perform his or her job for an hour. While there are some questions about the specifics of the job (e.g., where does the employee get his or her raw materials?), the hour is spent with relatively little structure being given to the observation other than watching the employee perform the job. The recording process, however, is highly structured. After the observation period is over, the observer fills out a 15-page instrument which requires that the observer rate the dimensions of the job using Likert-type items.

A third type of observation is *unstructured*. Here there are no specific directions regarding what should be observed and what should be recorded, or how. While unstructured observation (clinical or anthropological observation as it is frequently called) does not have an explicit structure, effective unstructured observation will usually have some kind of implicit underlying structure which at least directs the attention of the observer in general terms. Schein (1969), for example, in the first part of his book on process consultation provides a general framework for observing behavior in groups. By specifying the variables that should be considered (for example, communication and leadership), he provides a general structure for observation.

Advantages and Problems of Observation

The outstanding advantage of the observation process is it enables direct collection of data about behavior itself, rather than reports of behavior. As such, observational data have relatively high face validity. In other words, while people in the organization may doubt the validity of questionnaire responses and may attempt to deny the validity of interview data by arguing that people did not answer truthfully, well documented observational data have a great deal of strength and believability.

Observation collects data about behavior, rather than reports of behavior. Observation therefore enables one to discover existing patterns of behavior, which are not known to the people in the organization. Because of a lack of awareness, these data might never be revealed in a questionnaire. In addition, observation is a real-time data-collection device rather than a retrospective collection device. Self-reports mostly describe behavior that has occurred in the past, while observation deals with behavior that is occurring in the present. Retrospective reports frequently involve distortion. People tend to reinterpret earlier events in the light of what occurred later.

Finally, observation is an adaptive method. In all but the most structured observation schemes, the observer can modify what he or she is observing as the situation requires.

While valuable, observations also have a number of inherent logistical problems. As observations move away from the more structured forms (such as the Bales IPA), interpretation and coding must frequently be done in order to use the data. As with interviews, this interpretation and coding is expensive, takes time, and can be a source of further bias. Another problem that is often overlooked is that of sampling. In a questionnaire or interview, sampling may be an issue, but all it involves is deciding which respondents to pick and how many. Observations necessitate this sampling over people, but they also necessitate sampling over time (when should observations be done), sampling over space (where should the observer be located), and sampling over events (at what specific events in time should the observer be present). Less-structured observation also has a tremendous potential for observer bias and thus a requirement that observers be adequately trained so that different observers will see the same things when viewing an event. When all of these factors are added up (training, sampling, coding, etc.), effective observation becomes a potentially expensive proposition. However, many times there is simply no substitute for having a trained observer on the scene. Many important events or patterns of behavior cannot be understood without someone actually being present.

Using Observations

What becomes obvious is that simply entering an organization and observing things as they happen is significantly different from planned, systematic observation, be it structured, semi-structured, or unstructured. If the observational data are to be valid and useful, observations have to be planned for in advance. What to observe, how to observe, when and where to observe, and how to record must all be explicitly decided.

Since highly structured observational work is costly and requires a great deal of preparation, observation may best be used in situations where less-structured observational data may be usable. Observations, used skillfully, can be valuable validity checks on more extensive data collected through self-reports. Given the costs and problems of sampling, observation is probably most useful when the client system is relatively small—for example, when the client is a work team or group. In these cases, sampling becomes less critical since it is possible for the observer to be present during most critical events and to be in the presence of all relevant members most of the time.

A final concern is the effect the observer has on those being observed. While observation does not give the opportunity for response biases in the sense that interviews and questionnaires do, it is possible for people to be influenced to behave differently when observed than when not observed. In one case, the semi-structured job-observation scheme referred to above (Jenkins, Nadler, Lawler, and Cammann, 1975) was used to collect data on subordinate-supervisor interactions. Upon analysis, it was found that in over 900 hours of observation there were almost no interactions between the observed workers and their supervisors. After further investigation it became clear that this was not a normal pattern of behavior and that supervisors and workers alike avoided interaction while the worker was being observed. Thus, when using observations, the consultant needs to be aware of possible observer effects. This again underscores the need to clearly communicate to organization members the nature and rationale for different types of data collection.

SECONDARY DATA AND UNOBTRUSIVE MEASURES

Most of the methods that are used to gather data in organizations assume that data have not already been collected and thus must be obtained either by asking organizational members or by observation of events as they occur. In fact, organizations do an immense amount of data collection during the normal course of activities, and they therefore contain huge (but often hidden) "data banks," waiting to be used by the change agent. These data in general are called secondary data, since they are collected from secondary sources, rather than directly from the respondent. All data collected from sources other than the subject fall directly into this category. Another label for this class of data is *unobtrusive measures*. (The term is taken from Webb, Campbell, Schwartz, and Sechrest, 1966.)

In organizations, perhaps the richest source of secondary data is archives—that is, the various documents, records, and written material in the possession of the organization. These sources can be particularly valuable to the data collector.

Types of Secondary Data and Unobtrusive Measures

There are numerous types of secondary data and they vary from organization to organization. Mentioning a few common kinds of data should provide a picture of the range and potential usefulness of these measures. Many organizations, for example, keep detailed records of certain kinds of behavior including records of absenteeism, lateness, turnover, accidents, grievances, etc. Many of these data are collected for legal purposes and are therefore always available. Another kind of data is that which the organization collects about the performance of work units. In particular, data about productivity, reject rates, repairs, costs, complaints, etc. all provide information about the performance of the organization. Similarly, correspondence files may provide information on the number of meetings that are held and the nature of contacts between people and groups, both inside and outside the organization. Other kinds of records such as electric light bills, phone bills, sign in and sign out sheets for after hours work, etc. also are potential sources of useful information.

For the most part, the consultant will need to search the records and other sources relatively unaided by any structure or procedure. To a limited extent, work is being done on how to collect and quantify this kind of data so that it can be used for diagnosis, feedback, and evaluation in organizations. Macy and Mirvis (1976), for example, have developed a set of procedures to aid in the standardized collection of data on absenteeism, lateness, turnover, and similar behavior, and they have outlined steps for the assignment of dollar costs to such behavior. In other areas, however, the data collector will be on his or her own.

In the PNB case, the research team made extensive use of archival measures as part of the feedback system. Using the standardized procedures developed by Macy and Mirvis (1976), they were able to use company records to identify dollar costs associated with different levels of turnover and absenteeism within the bank branches. These data were incorporated into the feedback system so that each month the feedback report included not only the absenteeism rate for the branch, but also the estimated cost in dollars to the bank as a result of absenteeism and turnover. Putting a dollar figure on absenteeism served to make the consequences of the behavior tangible and also served to direct more attention to the absenteeism than it had earlier received.

Advantages and Problems with Secondary Data and Unobtrusive Measures

The advantages of secondary data are fairly obvious. Being unobtrusive, this type of data collection is relatively nonreactive. There is little chance for a response bias to occur due to the consultant's collection. In addition, archival data, especially those involving dollar figures, have extremely high face validity. As opposed to questionnaire, interview, or even most observational data, these data are "real" in the eyes of many people in the organization. Finally, most of these data are easily quantified and can thus be analyzed statistically.

The problems involved in using these data revolve around obtaining the data and assessing its validity. Access or retrieval is frequently a problem. An amazing number of organizations do not keep records of this kind in usable or retrievable form. For example, a consultant working with one firm found that while absenteeism data were kept on individuals for wage purposes, no aggregations were ever made, and obtaining absenteeism rates for units or departments was almost impossible. In the end, the consultant had to go through the individual absenteeism records manually, one by one, to get the data.

A second problem involves the potentially poor quality of much archival data. While archival data are usually accepted at face value within the organization, experiences with these measures suggest that frequently they bear little relation to reality. A consultant attempting to assess the effects of his or her interventions on job performance in a cereal plant, for example, began to collect data from the productivity records of the plant and from job-ticket information filled out by employees. Only after much frustrating analysis did the consultant discover that employees tended to randomly choose numbers to put on these tickets and that the numbers did not reflect actual production at all. Much of this distortion was indeed response bias—not to the consultant but to the normal data collection that goes on in the organization. People frequently provide the organization with the information that they think it wants or information that will reflect well on them, rather than information that is valid. (See Cammann and Nadler, 1976, for a discussion of why this occurs.)

Finally, archival data may pose problems of coding and interpretation. It's not always clear, for example, what constitutes an incident of absenteeism or lateness. The data can be interpreted in several different ways.

Issues in Using Secondary Data and Unobtrusive Measures

In general, archival data and unobtrusive measures are underused by consultants. There is a tendency to rely on one type of data, usually interviews or questionnaires, and sometimes observations, and to ignore the existence of data that have already been collected by the organization. These sources could be used much more than they have been.

Having decided to make use of archival data, it is important to check on the validity of the data so as to avoid the unfortunate incident described above which occurred with the job tickets. Here again, the consultant's internal partners and particularly a cross-sectional or labor-management group can be particularly helpful in guiding the consultant to valuable sources of data and steering him or her away from data that are generally known to be of dubious validity.

Collection of and access to data can be a problem. Checking correspondence files, employee folders, and signout lists (unless the reasons for this action are fully understood by the members of the organization), can cause a good deal of anxiety among members of the organization. In addition, once the data have been located they frequently are not in readily usable form (as in the absenteeism data example), and getting the data into usable form may involve expensive and tedious work with the organization's records.

Keeping this in mind, it is important to remember that this kind of data has an extremely high impact. Illustrating problems or changes in absenteeism rates, number of final assemblies rejected, or overtime charges can have an immense impact on both managerial and nonmanagerial people.

CHOOSING DATA-COLLECTION METHODS

As this discussion has emphasized, each method of data collection has its particular advantages as well as its specific drawbacks. While each situation may call for a different type of data-collection method, a few generalizations can be made about the use of different collection techniques.

One important suggestion is that consultants and managers always attempt to make use of a variety of different collection methods. The best way to compensate for the deficiencies of any one method is not to rely solely on that method for all of the data needed. One can avoid misinterpreting information or jumping to false conclusions by cross checking important pieces of information through other methods of data collection. For example, if a questionnaire indicates major problems around supervision in one department, it may be useful to interview some supervisors and nonsupervisory personnel in the specific department for more detailed information. It also may be valuable to spend some time in the department observing the interactions between supervisors and subordinates. The most effective data collection strategy, therefore, is one that uses multiple measures and multiple methods of data collection. It is by combining data from interviews, questionnaires, observations, and archival sources that the consultant is able to triangulate and thus discard the data that may be distorted or biased.

Despite the value of using multiple methods, some methods have very specific strengths in particular situations. As has already been mentioned, the questionnaire is a particularly useful method where a large organization composed of many employees is the client. The strategy in this case is to rely heavily on questionnaires, but to selectively use other data sources to check out or validate the critical findings from the questionnaire data.

In summary, the choice of data collection methods is an important one and a whole set of advantages and disadvantages for each method must be weighed against one another. While one cannot avoid making choices among these methods, the use of multiple data sources will help to avoid some of the most obvious and dangerous problems.

ANALYZING DATA AFTER COLLECTION

A well-known OD consultant made a presentation at a workshop, describing how he worked with organizations. In the course of his presentation, he handed out to the workshop participants copies of a questionnaire that he has used.

About six weeks later the following phone call took place:

Caller:	Hello.
Consultant:	Yes.
Caller:	You probably don't know me, but I was in a group that you spoke to about six weeks ago and I was very much impressed by your presentation.
Consultant:	Well, thank you.
Caller:	Yes, I was so impressed with your approach that I became convinced that our company needed to start taking a look at itself and make use of your methods.
Consultant:	Gee, that's terrific. It makes me feel good to know that people have found my ideas useful.
Caller:	That's right. It was so useful that I went ahead and used the questionnaire that you handed out to us. You remember that you said it wasn't copyrighted so we could use it?
Consultant:	Yes, I said that.
Caller:	So I got copies made and had everyone in my division, about 250 people, fill out and return the questionnaire to me.

Consultant:	That's good.
Caller:	Well now I'm sitting here in my office and I'm wondering. What do I do now?
Consultant:	What do you mean, what do I do now?
Caller:	I'm sitting here with the questionnaires and trying to figure out what kind of analysis to do. Do you have a regular set of procedures for using the questionnaire?
Consultant:	That depends. . . what kind of statistical packages do you have on your computer?
Caller:	What computer?
Consultant:	Oh my. Well you could start by getting means for the different scales on the questionnaire.
Caller:	What's a mean?

This conversation continued in the same vein for some time, until both the consultant and the caller became frustrated and decided to go their separate ways.

This case, while somewhat extreme, is typical of the kinds of problems that many encounter when using quantitative data for organizational change. It is relatively easy to collect data. It seems both logical and useful to administer a questionnaire, make observations, collect data from records, or conduct interviews and then "see what we come up with." While a tempting course of action, this approach clearly can lead to problems. Without the proper conceptual or technical tools, it is possible to swim around in data for days, weeks, or months without identifying important or critical characteristics of the information. Similarly, without proper planning for analysis before collection, one can find that the most critical question is the one that was never asked.

Assume, however, that the consultant and internal partners have been careful and have systematically prepared for data collection and feedback and have effectively collected data. Now faced with quantitative information, be it from questionnaires, coded interviews, or other sources, what should be done?

Basic Tools

Perhaps the most important issue in data analysis is the need for an analysis plan. In other words, both the consultant and his or her internal partners should have some idea of what they are going to do with the data after they have been collected. Data should be collected for a reason not just "because it's there," and analysis should be done with direction and purpose, not as a fishing expedition to "see what we come up with."

To do purposeful and effective data analysis, two very basic kinds of tools are needed. The first is the conceptual tool. Again, having some kind of model of behavior and organizational functioning is extremely important. Analysis is essentially a process of asking questions of the data, and therefore the analyst needs to have a set of questions in mind. In the case of organizational diagnosis and change, these questions are related to the health and functioning of an organization and should be based on some systematic way of thinking about organizations. As has been mentioned before, a good model provides a list of diagnostic questions which can serve as a roadmap—in this case a roadmap through the data.

The second type of tool is the technical tool. Specifically, there are techniques of analysis of quantitative data that enable the analyst to ask specific questions of a set of data to make sure that the answers are ones in which he or she can have reasonable confidence, and to assure that the patterns that are observed are true patterns and not due to chance.

Both of these kinds of tools are critical for working with data. Of the two, however, the conceptual tools are probably more important for data-based change because the models or frameworks that are used determine the basic approach to analysis. Correct technique with incorrect or inadequate questions may produce useless or misleading data. Once one knows what questions to ask, it is relatively easy to find the technical expertise to aid in asking those questions.

In summary, data analysis is made up of two components. The first component is an analysis provided by the consultant or developed by people in the organization. Such a model indicates what questions should be asked of the data. The second component is analysis techniques. These are no more than methods and procedures for asking questions of a set of data. (See Appendix A for a brief discussion of techniques and resources for data analysis.)

8
FEEDING BACK DATA

In the Northeastern Hospital case, the consultants did an excellent job of data collection and analysis. Both the content and the process of the data collection activities were carefully designed. Meetings were held with all work groups before data were collected. Data collection included questionnaires, interviews, observations, and collection from hospital records. Analyses were planned in advance and guided by the organizational model being used. The feedback report was carefully written and meetings were held to provide members of the organization with a clear picture of the data that had been collected.

With all of this work, the project failed to bring about any lasting significant changes in the way the organization functioned. Why did this happen? How could so much work and preparation lead to nothing? While there are obviously many responses to these questions, the basic answer is that feedback has to be more than just giving back information or reporting the results of data collection and analysis.

Feedback itself at best can only initiate change; it cannot bring it about. People in groups making use of feedback can create change. To understand how this happens, we must therefore be concerned with how to successfully use feedback in organizations. Successful use of feedback must be based on an understanding of how information changes behavior. According to theory and research, feedback can cause changes in behavior by the creation and direction of energy.

Energy must be both created (that is, aroused) and directed (guided towards certain goals). In addition, the effectiveness of different feedback mechanisms (disconfirmation, cueing, etc.) depends upon both the characteristics of the feedback and the characteristics of the process for using feedback.

Thus feedback does not automatically lead to change. As seen in Fig. 8.1, for feedback (or any intervention for that matter) to result in change, several questions must be addressed. The first question is whether the feedback creates any energy at all. If no energy is created, then there is no potential for change. People are not motivated to act, and thus change cannot occur. If energy is created, then the second question becomes important. What is the direction of the energy? Feedback can create energy to use data to identify and solve problems. On the other hand, feedback can be threatening and thus can create anxiety which leads to resistance and ultimately no change. Even if the feedback does create energy and direct it towards problem identification and solution, there is a third question of whether the means exist to transform that energy into concrete action. If not, frustration and failure may be experienced and no change will result. If those structures and processes do exist, then change can occur.

Given this set of questions, this chapter will address the questions of how to generate energy, how to direct energy, and how to facilitate the transformation of energy into concrete action. Several specific concerns will be examined. One is how to present data in a way that will create and direct energy. Another is how to provide for the use of data feedback so that energy will be created and directed. In particular, this relates to the nature of the feedback meeting, the forum where feedback data are presented and worked on. Finally, how should the entire process of feedback, use, and follow-up be structured so that energy will be transformed into action?

CRITERIA FOR EFFECTIVE FEEDBACK

At the core of the feedback process is the presentation of data to individuals. This presentation may be oral or written; it may be a single event or an ongoing process. Before considering the questions of how to present and work with data, it is thus important to think about the data itself. Specifically, what are the characteristics for effective feedback data?

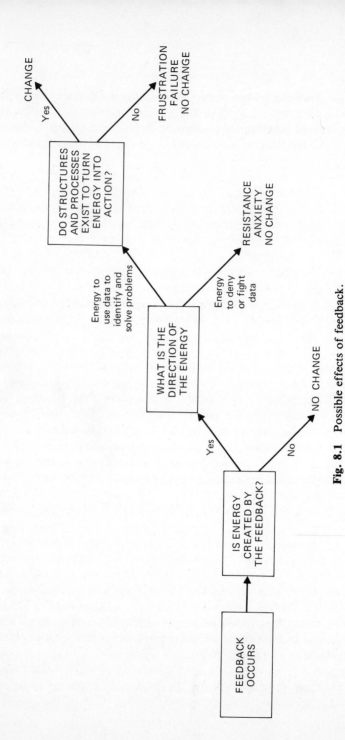

Fig. 8.1 Possible effects of feedback.

1. *Relevant.*   Information can only create energy if it relates to issues that are meaningful to the recipients. Information about those aspects of organizational behavior or functioning that have little relation to the lives of the people who receive the data usually will not create energy.

2. *Understandable.*   Frequently, data are presented in a way that makes them hard to understand. It is particularly important, therefore, that the form, language, and symbols used in feedback be familiar and understandable to the people in the organization.

3. *Descriptive.*   For feedback to generate energy, the receiver must be able to relate the data to real-life events in his world. Therefore, data need to be descriptive. They need to include enough real examples and illustrative detail so that people can relate to the information. Data that are very general leave the receiver with little to work with. The data should thus convey both the detail and the affect (feelings) that are part of the information collected.

4. *Verifiable.*   The theory says that people will respond more to data that they feel are valid and accurate. Thus the data in feedback need to be presented in a manner in which the receivers can validate the findings. For example, information might be presented on how the data were collected including how many interviews were conducted, what sampling procedures were used, etc. This kind of information enables the receiver to make his or her own judgment of whether the data are truly representative of what goes on in the organization.

5. *Limited.*   A major problem in the transmission of information to people is information overload. When too much information is presented, people become overwhelmed. Confusion and distortion occur and energy may be dissipated. People have limits to the amount of information that they can receive or process at one time. The temptation when giving feedback is to present great amounts of data. In reality, limited data organized to prevent overload are more effective at creating and directing energy.

6. *Impactable.*   Feedback should largely concern those areas of the organization that are under the control of the receiving group.

While there is value in providing information about the organization as a whole, most people can't do very much about the functioning of the whole organization. They can, however, do things that will affect the functioning of their own work unit or work group. Providing data about problems and issues out of the control of the receiving group may only lead to frustration and ultimately a decrease in energy. Presenting information that relates to the areas of activity that can be influenced by the receiver can, on the other hand, create energy to make changes that are truly possible to make.

7. *Comparative.* When feedback data are received, people go through their own process of evaluation, looking at those aspects of the organization that seem to be doing well in addition to problem areas. Feedback data, and particularly questionnaire data, are often ambiguous by nature, and it is often hard for organizational members to make their own evaluations and set their own priorities. Therefore, at least some part of the feedback data should include data that can serve as comparison points or bench marks. With this help, the receivers can determine whether the comparison is a valid one or not and make their own comparisons.

8. *Unfinalized.* Feedback data that imply that data collection is completed, that all problems have been identified, and that the work of diagnosis is finished only serve to decrease energy. In fact, successful use of feedback usually involves using the data as a starting point for further exploration rather than as an ending point. Feedback can only be a stimulus for action; it cannot economically present the entire picture of how an organization or even a part of an organization works. In a meeting, for example, the best and most descriptive data are in the heads of the people around the table, not on the feedback sheet of the consultant. For feedback to be effective, the formal data should serve only as a starting point for more in-depth data collection, problem identification, and problem solving.

PRESENTING DATA

In addition to the characteristics of the feedback data, the way in which data are presented is obviously important. The requirements that feedback should be understandable, descriptive, verifiable, and limited all relate to the issue of presentation. These criteria are important to keep in mind as two types of data presentation are considered: the presentation of quantitative data and the writing of feedback reports.

Presenting Quantitative Data

Having collected and analyzed data in quantitative form, it is often useful to present those data to people in the organization. Providing the actual data to people in the organization is consistent with a consulting strategy of sharing all relevant information with the client. The actual observable numbers are "hard" data which give the appearance of validity, have a potentially high impact, and are written testimony to the competence and expertise of the consultant as a data analyst. Presenting the data also provides the client with specific information to work on in depth.

On the other hand, the temptation to share data in its numerical form can sometimes overwhelm the considerations of good sense. Frequently, one sees consultants or researchers piling volume upon volume of computer output onto an overwhelmed, confused, but supposedly grateful client. Clients, or internal partners, are often the unwitting accomplices in the process, asking to see "all of the data."

The question then is how to present quantitative data, such as the results of questionnaire administrations or coded interviews or observations, in a usable form. A number of points should be kept in mind. First is the need to present only a limited amount of data. Although the entire set of data collected and/or analyzed can be made available to members of the organization, the formal presentation of data should be limited to those data that are particularly meaningful, as indicated by the nature of the group receiving the data, the nature of the results, and the nature of the organizational model used by the consultant to guide his or her analysis. Second, data should be presented in a format that is easy for the layman to read and interpret. All numbers should be clearly labeled; there should be only a limited amount of data on each page; extraneous statistical tests should not be a part of the presentation; and the meaning of the numbers should be interpretable from the presentation. As such, the data presentation should be self-contained. Finally, it is often helpful to have some kind of graphic display of the data. This is particularly useful when there are comparisons of any kind such as over time or across samples.

Drawing a picture from the data can often help people to see trends or patterns of results.

There obviously are many different ways of presenting data, and only the most basic issues in presentation are discussed here. These principles of presentation, however, are applicable to a broad range of data feedback activities. An example of one type of computer generated data presentation format (based on a group process questionnaire) is included in Appendix B.

Data presentation can be aided by some work with the receivers of the data before the feedback actually takes place. For example, it may be useful to have the clients decide in advance what data they want to look at and what kinds of questions they will want to ask of the data. This kind of activity helps the receivers of feedback to focus their attention ahead of time while also giving the consultant information on what data to include in the feedback and what data can possibly be excluded from the primary presentation. Similarly, it may be worthwhile to orient people to the nature and format of the data presentation before they receive feedback.

Written Feedback Reports

There are times when a written report describing the results of the data collection is desirable. A written document gives the members of the organization something tangible to work with. It can serve as a working tool for further data collection and problem identification. People can take the report, examine it in detail, and come up with their own conclusions. It therefore provides the opportunity for more comprehensive and in-depth work with the data by the members of the organization. Similarly, it provides an alternative way of communicating the data to those who, for one reason or another, cannot be present at any oral presentation. Finally, it provides a verifiable description of the data. Such a description cannot be distorted later on, as an oral presentation might be.

At the same time, it is important to realize that a written feedback report is not a substitute for some kind of live meeting to hear and work with the data. As will be seen, most of the research and experience with data-based methods indicates that significant changes occur only when meetings are held to work with the data. The feedback report can be a useful supplement, but it is not a substitute for an effective live process of working with the information.

As with data presentations, there are important factors to consider concerning how the report communicates its content to the organizational members. Again, information overload is a persistent problem. Consultants frequently like to show their work and impress clients by providing mammoth feedback reports with slick covers, well designed charts, numerous appendices, and a thick and thoughtful text. Experience indicates, however, that most people will not read such a report and only a few will bother even to attempt to go through this kind of document in detail. Thus a short report which provides a limited amount of information in a clear and concise manner is a much more effective device for communicating information and stimulating people to think about the data.

Even with a short report, some people may not have the time or patience to read an entire written report. For these people, it is often valuable to start the report with a brief (for example, one page) written overview of the entire report that highlights the major points and findings. Similarly, the report should be clearly organized so that people can turn to those areas that are of concern to them and find the data and discussions that interest them without wading through other less relevant material.

The report is often a good place to describe how the data were collected and analyzed. By providing this information, the organization's members have a chance to verify and/or validate the data. By looking at the procedures used for collection and analysis they can decide for themselves whether the data provide a valid picture of the organization.

In summary, the report should provide people in the organization with enough information to work with, while not providing too much information. There should be data in enough detail so that individuals can begin to clearly identify major problems and some of their causes as well as follow up by collecting their own data through group discussions or explorations. Data, however, should be limited so that information overload does not occur.

THE FEEDBACK MEETING

Both the research and experience with data-based change point to the importance of the feedback meeting (Klein, Kraut, and Wolfson, 1971; Nadler, 1976). Very clearly, change begins to occur when people sit down together to work with the data. What goes on at feedback meetings is thus at the center of the question of whether feedback will produce change.

Change is initiated or occurs in two different ways in the feedback meeting. First, change occurs as a result of attention to the *content* of the data that are being fed back. As described in Chapter 4, by providing data, behavioral change can occur through mechanisms such as disconfirmation, learning, cueing, etc. The data provide information on problems in the organization and can thus trigger problem identification and solving. The data also provide people with goals to work toward and rewards for doing well. Thus the content of the data—what the data actually say—is an important and obvious factor for initiating change.

A second important aspect of the feedback meeting, however, relates to the *process* of making use of data to identify and solve problems. Most approaches to feedback involve using the feedback meeting not only to examine what problems exist and what solutions may be applicable, but also to examine *how* the group goes about working and solving problems. The meeting is used to learn about and improve how the group works together, often with the help of an outside consultant.

The process and content dimensions of the feedback meeting are related to each other. A successful feedback meeting needs to be effective on both dimensions. Process is particularly helpful in aiding the group in working through content problems. On the other hand, process problems in the group may only be symptomatic of larger problems as reflected in the content of the feedback data. Both elements are important.

Having dealt earlier with how the content of feedback creates change, the important question is how to create an effective process in feedback meetings so that energy will be generated, directed, and transformed into action.

Process Issues in Feedback Meetings

Any group attempting to do work faces problems of building an effective process (see Schein, 1969). Thus a group specifically meeting to work on feedback has the normal process concerns of leadership, participation, communication, power, decision making, etc. The feedback situation, however, has certain special aspects which make it a problematic environment in which to work. As the meeting begins, people are about to receive data that pertain to themselves and possibly their own behavior. This is a very different situation from that of working with everyday information that may deal with things like production, markets, or issues that focus away from the behavior of the group. Because of this, the experience may be uncomfortable; people may hear things that are not favorable. These may be things that they may not want to hear at first. Because of this, individuals walk into feedback meetings with a number of different kinds of feelings that clearly affect the process of the meeting:

1. *Anxiety.* Perhaps the most pervasive feeling is one of anxiety. In organizations, most individuals do not usually give, receive or hear valid and straightforward feedback. Therefore, a feedback meeting is a new, unusual, and frequently uncertain situation. People do not know what to expect. This uncertainty makes the feedback meeting an initially uncomfortable experience. It is not clear what is happening or what will happen, and this causes people to be anxious.

2. *Defensiveness.* Specifically, people enter the meeting thinking about the possibility that negative things might be said about them, either individually or as a group. They therefore are ready to defend themselves against attack. This defensiveness clearly can get in the way of effective communication and can hinder the ability of the group to identify and solve problems. When people are more interested in defending themselves than finding out the causes of and responses to problems, it becomes difficult to do constructive work.

3. *Fear.* People also worry about the consequences of feedback. If, for example, lower level employees have filled out a questionnaire and have been critical of their supervisor, they may be concerned about his or her reaction to the questionnaire results. They may fear his or her response, seeing the possible results as being decreased communication and punishing behavior. Fear concerning the reactions of other people, particularly people in power, creates expectations that openness by individuals will only lead to negative outcomes. It therefore motivates people to be cautious, to hedge on their positions, and in some cases to not participate at all. When people enter a meeting with some fear, the real issues may lurk beneath the surface, never being raised up.

4. *Hope.*   Not all of the feelings that people have upon entering the meeting are negative. Frequently, individuals come to feedback meetings with a great deal of excitement and positive energy. They see in the data and in the meetings the possibility of major and constructive change. They see an opportunity for critical information to be put on the table, for problems to be brought to the surface, and for problem solving to begin. This is seen in high levels of energy, and in a feeling of hope that the meetings will bring about positive change.

To some degree, group members and leaders come to the meetings with a combination of each of these feelings. The fact, however, that people come into the meeting with strong feelings of anxiety, defensiveness, fear, and hope makes the feedback meeting a particularly complex situation and implies that issues of process in the group are important if the group is to do constructive work. There are many opportunities for the group to get side-tracked, to spend its energy in defensive or punitive behavior, or to let anxiety serve as a blockage to effective action. The process of working with the data is therefore important.

What Usually Happens in a Feedback Meeting

What can one expect to occur in the feedback meeting? In any meeting there is both a formal agenda as well as an informal process of group development. Looking first at the formal agenda of the feedback meeting, several specific approaches have been outlined elsewhere in detail. (See for example, IBM, 1974; or Hausser, Pecorella, and Wissler, 1975, for detailed guides on how to run a meeting.) Most formal outlines see the meeting as having several discrete phases. Frequently, there is pre-meeting preparation with the meeting leader (sometimes the supervisor of a work group) or with the leader and the consultant. During the meeting itself, the first step is a brief introduction where the group leader or consultant attempts to describe the goals of the meeting and to establish how the group will work together. Second, the leader or consultant gives a presentation or overview of the data. Third, the group gets involved in specific parts of the data, working to identify and define problems and develop solutions. This stage may extend over many meetings. Finally, the solutions that are generated are put into some kind of action plan as a basis either for recommendations or actual concrete action that will be taken.

While it is possible to outline a formal agenda for a feedback meeting, other events occur in the meeting that are not accounted for by the formal structure of the meeting. Neff (1965) has provided some insight into what happens at the meeting by describing a series of stages that groups receiving feedback appear to go through. Although this is a general description, it may be helpful in understanding some of the behavior that occurs.

The first stage concerns *data validity*. People enter the meeting anxious and defensive, and possibly skeptical of the ability of the consultant's data-collection methods to come up with anything substantial or new. A frequent pattern in such meetings is early denial of the validity of the data. So the initial process issue is whether the people at the meeting will accept the data as being valid and accurate. Thus it is crucial early in the meeting to present data that people can verify, to provide them with some information on how the data were obtained, and to create a climate in the group so that people will not be motivated to deny the validity of the data. Obviously, if organizational members have been highly involved in the data collection and analysis, many of the validity problems have been taken care of.

Once the validity of the data has been established, a second issue becomes important. Specifically, the group members may resist *accepting responsibility* for the data and what they represent. They may claim that the results do not apply to their group or that the causes of problems lie elsewhere (top management, etc.). Frequently, this is "flight" behavior which members engage in to avoid the uncomfortable task of dealing with the problems indicated by the data. Here the role of the consultant or leader is important to help the group redirect its energies toward identifying those aspects of its behavior for which it is responsible and away from flight or blaming other groups or individuals for problems.

Only when the data have been accepted as valid and the group has accepted the responsibility for the data can *problem solving* occur. Problem solving involves some version of the basic steps of defining the problem, collecting information, generating alternative solutions, evaluating alternative solutions, making a choice of action plans, and implementing action plans. (For a detailed description of problem solving processes in groups, see Morris and Sashkin, 1976.)

The role of the consultant and group leader (who may or may not be the same person) is thus one of helping the group to resolve major issues of validity and responsibility so that it can move through the first two stages and begin problem solving. If the group is not helped, it may become "stuck" at one of the stages and never get to the point of accepting responsibility for problems and action.

What's Necessary to Make a Meeting Work Well

Assuming that most groups working with feedback will have normal process problems, will face the particular concerns of anxiety, defensiveness, hope and fear, and will in some form move through the stages that Neff (1965) outlines, what is needed to make a meeting work well? What things should be present to ensure that the group will effectively work on identifying and solving problems, that people will communicate clearly, that the process issues that may get in the way of the work will be surfaced, and that some kind of action steps will be generated from the meeting?

Assume that planning and preparation have been done well, that data collection and analysis have been competently executed, and that the feedback data and/or reports are presented well. Some energy has already been generated through the planning, data collection, and analysis work. It is now time to hold meetings with the purpose of generating more energy, of directing that energy, and transforming that energy into concrete action that will result in the improvement of the organization. Given all of this, the meeting must have at least some of the following characteristics if it is to be successful.

1. *Motivation to Work with the Data.*   People must be motivated to work with the feedback information. They need to feel that working on the data will lead to positive results. These results may come from the activity itself. For example, people may feel that working on the data will lead to an improved organization or working life. People may also be motivated by specific rewards. For example, a person may feel that his or her supervisor will approve of attempts to use the data to solve problems. Frequently, however, people feel that if they work on the data, raise problems, or attempt to identify their concerns, they will be punished by the organization or by their supervisor in some way. If people come into a meeting with the feeling that any raising of problems will be punished, their motivation to work on the data will be decreased, and participation in the meeting may be very low. This underscores the need for early planning, understanding, and commit-

ment of power groups to the data collection and feedback process. If the general perception is that management, for example, does not really want to find out about and work on problems, all the meetings in the world may lead to nothing.

2. *Assistance in Using the Data.* In the group, there must be some skill in using the data. Specifically, someone in the group needs to understand how the data were collected, what they mean, and how they should be interpreted. In addition, there should be skill in using data once they are understood. Someone in the meeting needs to know what to do with the feedback. This person (or persons) may be a group member, the formal leader, or someone from outside the group who can serve as a consultant to the group.

3. *A Structure for the Meeting.* The feedback meeting is a new experience for many people in the organization. In other meetings they have structures such as procedures, agendas, rules, or ways of working together that they are used to. Working with feedback is a new kind of task and the old structures may not be adequate for this kind of task. Therefore, it may be useful to have an agenda or outline which can serve as a guide to how to go about working with the data. Such an agenda provides some guidance or a road map for the group to follow.

4. *Appropriate Membership.* An important issue is who should attend the meeting. In general, people who have problems in common and can benefit from working together on questions raised by the data should attend the meeting. Who these people are, however, may vary from situation to situation. In some cases this may be a formal work unit with its supervisor, a work unit without its supervisor, or a new group which cuts across existing lines. Different types of problems and different approaches to feedback call for different groups. Specific types of groups will be discussed below. The important point is that thought should be given to who are to be group members.

5. *Appropriate Power.* Related to membership is the question of power. Specifically, does the group that works with the feedback have any power to make changes? Can it do anything or is the feedback session merely an exercise in "what we would like to do if we could do

it"? The feedback group needs to have a clear idea of its power. On what issues can it make changes, on what issues can it recommend changes, and what issues are clearly out of its domain? A feedback group that has no power to make any changes may be better off not meeting at all. Of course, not every group can have the power to re-structure the entire organization, but groups can be provided with power to change how they work together and to alter certain aspects of their environments. Again the need is to clarify the nature of the group's power and to focus the efforts of the group toward those areas over which it can exercise some control. For the total organiza-tion to change, some structure must be set up to ensure that the results of the feedback-initiated problem solving will get translated into con-crete action.

6. *Process Help.*   A final needed factor is some kind of assistance to ensure that the group's process is at least minimally effective. Someone, either inside or outside of the group, needs to be attuned to the various process issues—to be watching *how* the group is working, rather than what it is working on. This should be a person who has the skills to intervene and help the group to improve its process as it works on real organizational problems.

SYSTEMATIC APPROACHES TO FEEDBACK AND FEEDBACK MEETINGS

There is no one best way to structure and conduct a feedback meeting. Over the past few years different approaches to feedback in organiza-tions have been developed. While most of them relate to survey feed-back, the ideas are obviously applicable to feedback of all different kinds of data. What is important is that each approach is a systematic, preplanned, and tested way of structuring feedback activities. Each attempts to deal with the question of how to ensure that the process and content of the feedback meetings will be effective and that ideas will be turned into concrete action. A few of the major approaches, or feedback designs, are as shown in Table 8.1.

Family Group Survey Feedback

One of the first systematic approaches to feedback was the family group survey feedback approach developed by Floyd Mann and his

Table 8.1

Major systematic approaches to feedback and feedback meetings

Approach	Major features
Family group survey feedback	Feedback to family group (work group and its supervisor) Data are questionnaire based Group gets process help from consultant
Survey-guided development	Feedback to family groups in a waterfall Attitude data based on a model Process help from trained internal resource people Systemic diagnosis of total system
Subordinate group	Feedback to family group Subordinates see data first, work on it before supervisor sees it Subordinates then meet with supervisor
Peer group–intergroup	Peer groups see data and work on it by themselves concurrently Cross level meetings then held. (vertical intergroup)
Intergroup	Feedback shared between groups Meetings held with both groups to work on problems (horizontal intergroup)
Collateral problem-solving group	Separate feedback, problem solving, and decision making structure set up outside of normal structure. Collateral group does data collection, feedback, and problem solving.
Ad hoc collateral groups	Feedback given to large group Small action groups form around problems
Ongoing feedback	Collection of feedback at regular intervals Technical and attitude data

colleagues at the Institute for Social Research of the University of Michigan (Mann, 1957; Mann and Likert, 1952; Baumgartel, 1959). At the core of this approach is the collection and feedback of data to what are called *family groups* within the organization. A family group is a formal work group made up of a supervisor and all the people that directly report to him or her. Implicit in this approach is the assumption that the critical behavioral problems in organizations are related to issues of leadership and group functioning (Likert, 1961) and that the formal work group is the most logical forum for working on these problems. As opposed to other possible groups, such as a T-group made up of people who do not work with each other, the family group can implement solutions to problems because it is the group that actually works together in the day-to-day situation. An important element in the family group survey feedback model is the process consultant. While feedback sessions might be conducted by the formal leader or supervisor, a consultant is present to help the work group to solve problems. The consultant aids the group by calling the group's attention to process problems, and in particular process issues having to do with how the group goes about problem solving. As a result, the group receiving feedback works on the data, but at the same time works on developing its own ability as a problem solving group.

Survey Guided Development

A logical extension of the family group survey feedback approach is the survey guided development design developed by Bowers and Franklin (1972; 1976). Survey guided development is an extension and refinement of the survey feedback concept, drawing heavily on Likert's (1961; 1967) model of organizational functioning. As with survey feedback, the core of survey guided development is the feedback of questionnaire data to formal work groups (family groups) within the organizations. Several important differences exist, however, between the two different approaches.

Survey guided development explicitly uses a top-down approach. Feedback starts with the top work group in the organization and then proceeds downward in what is called a "waterfall" design. Each supervisor participates as a group member in a feedback session with his or her manager and peers before conducting a feedback session with his or her subordinates. As the feedback process moves downward through the hierarchy, ideas and suggestions are filtered upwards through the chain of work groups. Second, the attitude data are taken from a standardized survey based on the Likert model (Taylor and Bowers, 1972). Third, process help and skill in using the data do not come from outside consultants. Rather a group of internal resource people who are organizational members are trained in the concepts of the model and techniques of survey feedback. These internal people then serve as resources in the family group meetings. Finally, the waterfall feedback design is supplemented by what is called "systemic diagnosis." The outside consultants write up a comprehensive analysis of the problems and functioning of the total organization based on the questionnaire results and give this report to top management. Based on the group feedback meetings and the systemic diagnosis, the organization may then go beyond survey feedback and begin other intervention work (such as job design, changes in compensation systems, etc.).

Subordinate Group Feedback

Another variation on the family-group approach has been suggested by Schein (1976). Using the family group has risks because of the possibility of conflict between the role of the supervisor as leader of the meeting and the role of supervisor as a possible focus for feedback as a potential cause of problems. The supervisor may do things that hinder the group's ability to work with the data. Schein offers an alternative to the "top-down" survey guided development approach with a "bottoms-up" subordinate group approach. In this case subordinates in the family group receive the feedback and work with it before the supervisor ever sees the data. The group works with the data with the assistance of a consultant. Only after considerable work has been done is the supervisor given the data and then asked to join the meeting. Thus by the time the supervisor does join the meeting the data have been validated; the group feels some ownership over the data; and the process of using the data as a problem-identification and problem-solving tool has been started. Much of the initial anxiety, fear, and defensiveness is diffused by having the supervisor absent.

Peer Group-Intergroup Feedback

Similar concerns with the effect of the supervisor in the feedback meeting have led to the development and testing of another approach, the peer group intergroup design (Heller, 1970; Alderfer and Holbrook, 1973). In this design, groups of peers (people at the same organizational level) review the data separately. Subordinates in one group therefore work with the data in the absence of their supervisor. At the same time, however, the supervisor works with the data in his or her peer group (with other supervisors at the same level). After working in peer groups, with consultative help, the groups are brought together to share perceptions and work on problems. Again the process of using the data and working on potentially threatening issues is initiated in the relatively safe peer-group environment and only later moved to the meeting with superiors. The final stage is essentially an intergroup conflict resolution meeting, with the groups arrayed along a vertical dimension, one group being the subordinate of another group.

Intergroup Feedback

Although not exclusively a feedback approach, intergroup confrontation meetings, such as those proposed by Beckhard (1969), are applicable to the use of feedback. Data concerning the relations between two or more groups are collected by various means, either by questionnaire, individual interview, or a direct group interview. Included in these data are perceptions of one group by another group. These data are then fed back to the other group as a way of initiating a discussion of the conflicts, tensions, and common interests that exist among the groups.

Collateral Problem Solving Groups

One of the arguments that has been made is that the family group is not the most effective place for receiving feedback and working on problems. The family group with its supervisor is part of the hierarchy of the organization. Frequently, the problems that the feedback deals with are caused by the nature of the organization's structure and how it solves problems. To expect that structure to do an effective job of working on itself may be unrealistic. Based on this observation, a number of feedback designs have been developed which involve the creation of new structures outside of the existing hierarchy to be special feedback, problem solving, and decision-making groups.

Probably the best developed example of this is the collateral problem-solving group design developed for use in educational settings (Coughlan and Cooke, 1974; Mohrman, Duncan, and Cooke, 1975). The basic feature is the creation of new groups outside the current structure. These groups include representatives of the organization's (in this case the individual school's) members. Similar groups are created at other levels of the organization (for example, at the level of the school district). These groups have overlapping membership so that communication across levels of the new hierarchy is relatively easy and so that groups at the school level can refer broader problems and receive support from groups at a higher (district) level.

In each group, at least one member receives intensive training on problem solving and survey feedback methods from outside consultants. This individual subsequently serves as the process consultant and group leader. The group then coordinates the collection of data, and the feedback is directed to this group. The group works to solve problems, make decisions, and implement solutions with the help of other groups at different levels. Thus feedback is used as an initiator. The groups are permanent structures which become involved in other kinds of change and frequently resort to other kinds of data collection activities and interventions. The design combines feedback with the creation of a new organizational structure to build a permanent mechanism for identifying and solving problems in the organization, this mechanism being outside of the basic formal organizational structure. As a permanent structure it has the advantage of continuing change activities long after the first survey and feedback sessions.

Ad Hoc Collateral Groups

A variation of the collateral group design is the creation of multiple collateral groups, each focused on a specific problem or issue and each having a temporary or limited existence. This ad hoc design (Nisberg, 1976) involves less of a radical change in the organization's structure, but still involves the creation of some mechanisms outside of the existing structure designed for identifying and solving problems. Typically, feedback from a survey is given to a large organizational unit (such as a division or a large department). This feedback can be given in multiple sessions or in one large session. In the course of the feedback presentation, critical issues and problems are identified. Following feedback, small groups are formed through self-selection. Each of these small "action groups" is charged with working on a specific problem surfaced by the feedback (such as supervision, pay system, etc.). These groups may conduct further data collection and develop action plans. These plans are then put together by the consultant and used as a basis for deciding on further steps including additional data collection, further feedback, or other changes in the organization.

Ongoing Feedback

Another variation in feedback design involves a change in the technology of the data collection and feedback, rather than the process by which it is used. The basic concept is that survey feedback can be combined with the features of ongoing control systems in organizations to create ongoing feedback systems (Nadler, Mirvis, and Cammann, 1976). (Also see the PNB case in Chapter 2 for an example of such an approach.) Data are collected on a regular basis (such as monthly or quarterly) and fed back relatively soon after collection. The data include both survey data as well as other measures of organizational functioning (productivity, quality measures, absenteeism and turnover, etc.). The system is designed by a representative group within the organization and the data are distributed to everybody in a particular work unit.

Ongoing feedback is no more than a technology change. It can thus be used in conjunction with other feedback processes such as family groups, subordinate groups, or collateral groups.

SUMMARY

Choosing Feedback Designs

The different feedback designs that have been presented each have their advantages and disadvantages. Some build on the existing organizational structures while others combine feedback with structural change in the organization. Some designs envision feedback as an end in itself, as the major organizational change intervention, while others see feedback as merely a diagnostic technology leading to other kinds of substantive changes. Some are based on highly detailed organizational models, while others are more narrowly focused towards specific techniques. Finally, the designs presented here represent only a few of the many possible feedback designs. Other approaches exist and many more await to be developed and articulated.

As we will see in the final chapter, there is a growing realization that no one feedback design is best for all situations. The consultant, the manager, and the organization need to choose the design that offers the best combination of cost and benefits and that best fits the goals of the larger change efforts in the organization. On one end of the spectrum, "top-down" family group feedback has rather modest change goals, while the collateral problem-solving group is a major structural intervention in itself and holds the promise for highly visible major change. In each case, however, the organization needs to make a conscious choice of the kind of feedback design it needs and should then do what is necessary to make that design work. In most cases, this boils down to having the necessary process assistance either from outside consultants or through the training and development of internal resource people.

Creating and facilitating a feedback process that will bring about change is a complex task and its description could encompass a book in itself. (For one excellent description specifically using the survey guided development design, see Hausser et al., 1975.) In addition to the specific questions dealt with here, some basic themes have again reappeared. The feedback process needs to be planned for in advance, preferably with members of the organization involved. Feedback is more effective if the data are based on some underlying model and the people receiving the feedback have some knowledge of that model. How feedback will be used is important, and the skills of aiding a group in using feedback are critical. Feedback is only a tool, not a full intervention program in itself. It can, if used effectively, create and direct energy, but comprehensive change may often require additional interventions. Finally, feedback designs, as with any other kind of intervention, should be developed in response to the needs and nature of the particular organization, implying that different organizations will require different kinds of feedback designs.

PART 4
CONCLUSION

9
PERSPECTIVES AND NEW DIRECTIONS

Our knowledge about using data-based methods for organization development is still very limited. This book has attempted to take what we know and bring it together into a coherent discussion; the discussion has built on the concept of a data-collection/feedback cycle common to all data-based interventions. At each stage, attempts have been made to draw from both experience and research to identify critical issues and to describe different ways that practitioners might respond to these issues.

In this last chapter we will be taking a step back to gain some perspective on the general issue of using data for organizational change. We will be concerned with what the research tells us about the usefulness and effectiveness of data-based methods. In addition we will be concerned with possible directions for future efforts.

WHAT DO WE KNOW ABOUT USING DATA FOR CHANGE?

Since the early days of the first survey feedback programs, there has been a growing amount of research conducted in organizations aimed at understanding the use and impact of data-based methods. Some of this research has been concerned with evaluating the effects of data-based change efforts. (See, for example, Miles, Hornstein, Callahan, Calder and Schiavo, 1969; McElvaney and Miles, 1971; Callahan and Lake, 1973; Brown, 1972; Bowers, 1973.) Other work has focused on the process issues in data-based change, and in particular on how the process of using data may affect the ultimate impact of a data-based change program. (See, for example, Chesler and Flanders, 1967; Klein, Kraut, and Wolfson, 1971; Alderfer and Ferris, 1972; Alderfer and Holbrook, 1973.) The specific results and implications of this research have been detailed elsewhere (Nadler, 1976). What is important to the practitioner is that a number of general observations and implications emerge from this body of research. Although the bulk of the work is focused on the use of survey feedback, the implications appear to be generalizable across the whole range of possible data-based methods.

Feedback Does Have Some Positive Effects

Most of the work reveals that feedback interventions do lead to positive changes in the organization. It is important to note, however, that the positive effects are uneven and inconsistent. Despite the caution, it seems that collecting and feeding back data to members of an organization can be an effective approach to change. Feedback in different cases has been associated with changes in employee attitudes and perceptions as well as changes in specific and observable behaviors in the organization. Thus the potential for change exists.

How Feedback is Used is an Important Factor

As we have stressed throughout this book, the way in which the data collection and feedback activities are conducted, the *process* of feedback, is of major importance. Where there has been an effective and active process for using the data, such as frequent meetings, intensive training, or specific structures for using feedback, then positive changes tend to occur. Similarly, the greater the participation by members of the organization in the entire collection-feedback process, the more change comes from the data. Many of the uneven results can be accounted for by variation in how the data were collected, analyzed, and fed back.

Feedback Seems Most Effective When Combined with Other Interventions

Our view of organizations and change implies that one specific change (for example, a data-collection and feedback activity) will not necessarily lead to significant and lasting changes in the way that the organization functions. It is therefore not surprising to find that feedback by itself may be a very limited change tool. Where feedback interventions have been the only ones used, the effects have tended to be limited or short-term in nature. However, when feedback has been combined with other kinds of interventions (such as the collateral group structure mentioned in the last chapter) the effects seem to be stronger and longer-lasting. Data are one kind of tool, a tool that is most effective when used in conjunction with other appropriate change technologies.

There is No One Best Feedback Design

A number of different feedback designs were discussed earlier. The research and experience suggest that different situations may call for different kinds of feedback designs. In particular, evidence exists that where there are different kinds of work processes or technologies, different feedback designs are appropriate (Sashkin and Cooke, 1976). Experience indicates different organizations with different kinds of employees, tasks, roles, and work processes, may require different approaches to feedback.

The research therefore gives us some help by suggesting that data-based methods (in general) and feedback (specifically) are potentially effective tools; that the process of using data is an important factor influencing how effective they will be; that feedback is most effective when combined with different interventions; and that different situations require different feedback designs. At this time, however, we are only beginning to define some of the specific techniques and approaches that will enable people in organizations to make the best choices among alternative interventions, feedback processes, and feedback designs. For the present, these choices have to be made on the basis of experience rather than on the basis of any hard or objective criteria.

NEW DIRECTIONS

With some perspective on what we already know about using data in organizations, it becomes clear that there are many areas where further work is needed by both researchers and practitioners. A few areas are worth particular attention.

Clearly, one major need is for more work on the question of what kinds of feedback designs are most appropriate for different situations. We know that different situations may demand different designs, but we are not sure what kinds of situations and what kinds of designs. Tied in with this is the need to experiment and develop new types of feedback designs. We need to go beyond the designs we have now and think of new and imaginative ways to combine data-based methods with other types of interventions to build new hybrid change technologies.

A second need is to increase our willingness and abilities to use data other than questionnaire data. Most of the work and almost all of the research on data-based change has centered on the use of the structured organizational survey. As has been pointed out, there are many other rich, useful, and accessible sources of valid data within organizations. There are also strong arguments which support using multiple sources of data to get the best and most valid picture of how the organization functions. A challenge then is to make better use of these kinds of data and to develop techniques and designs which incorporate a broad range of data, rather than rely solely on the results of a questionnaire.

More attention should be given to the question of how to use feedback. Much of the work to date has been concentrated on developing the technology of data-based change, such as questionnaires, models, and designs, as opposed to identifying and developing the skills that will be useful in making data-based methods work. Specifically, we need to identify what skills are critical to make feedback meetings effective. We also need to figure out how to develop those skills within the organization.

The ultimate test of the usefulness of data-based methods, as with any change approach, is the extent to which an organization can learn to use the tools and concepts on its own, without extensive and continuing help from outside consultants. This would indicate that an area for future work is in developing ways of transferring the technology and expertise of data-based methods to the organization, so that the organization can do its own data collection, analysis, and feedback work. Some work has already begun in this direction (Bowers and Franklin, 1976), but other approaches and models need to be developed. One ultimate goal is the creation of continuing feedback loops in organizations. Healthy and adaptive organizations should be continually collecting and using data to identify and solve problems. Through control systems and other similar mechanisms, many organizations attempt to do this with regards to the technical systems of the organization. They collect data about markets, raw materials, technical performance, etc., and use that information to solve problems and make decisions. Thinking of information in terms of organizational behavior and change offers the potential of extending the scope and impact of these systems. One could envision an organization where the collection and feedback of data about the human processes and systems is as much a part of the central activity of the organization as the budgeting cycle or the maintenance of inventory levels. The image of using data-based methods to build self-correcting and adaptive human systems is an exciting one. Again, initial attempts have been made (Nadler, Cammann, and Mirvis, 1976), but much more remains to be done.

SUMMARY

In our exploration of data-based methods and their use, certain themes have been repeated over and over. In summary, it may be useful to touch on them for one last time. One central theme has been the importance of data-based tools and processes to organization development. The collection and feedback of data is a central part of any effective OD activity. Improving organizations through participative processes implies the need to collect data about how the organization functions at present and to give the data in some form to people in the organization so that they can work with it and ultimately use the information for problem solving.

Second, we have stressed that information is a tool. As such it has both the power and limitations of any tool—it can be effective if used well and possibly destructive if used poorly. It is no more effective or destructive than the people (both in and outside of the organization) who use it. As a tool it also has inherent limitations to its usefulness. No one specific tool is applicable in all situations or is the correct one to use all of the time. It needs to be used with judgment and in conjunction with other tools as appropriate.

Data are a potentially powerful source of energy for change. Information about *what is* can be a potent force that moves people towards *what should be*. It is through valid pictures of ourselves that we develop images of where we can and would like to be. This is particularly critical for planned change in organizations. Organization development is a process of learning. We are attempting to build organizations that can learn about themselves—organizations that can learn to make themselves more effective. Learning cannot take place in the absence of information. Through systematic collection and use of data in organizations, we may be able to take at least small steps towards improving organizations, toward making them more effective, and towards making them better places for people to work.

APPENDIXES

APPENDIX A
SOME ELEMENTARY
TECHNIQUES FOR DATA ANALYSIS

Data analysis techniques are useful in helping the consultant and others in the organization to ask questions of a set of data that have been collected. For example, having collected a large amount of questionnaire data from an organization, one might want to ask the question, "Are people satisfied in this organization?" Following up, one might look to the data to find the answer to the questions, "Which people are more satisfied than others?" or "Is there any relationship between level in the hierarchy and satisfaction?" Analysis techniques are simply ways of asking such questions and getting answers.

In this brief appendix, analysis will be looked at from two perspectives. First, a number of specific data analysis techniques will be discussed and illustrated. Second, several sources of readily available expertise for data analysis in organizations will be identified.

It is extremely important to caution the reader that this discussion cannot adequately describe all of the tools, techniques, and assumptions that go into competent data analysis. All that can be done is to describe a few techniques and thus give some intuitive feel for how analysis is conducted. Those who are contemplating doing their own analysis should consult some of the many sources of detailed information about how to work with quantitative data. (See, for example, Hays, 1963; or Nie, Hull, Jenkins, Steinbrenner, and Bent, 1975.)

TECHNIQUES

There are a few simple techniques that can be used to begin to understand quantitative data. These techniques are basically ways of describing and summarizing a set of data. With small samples, these can be done by hand or by a desk calculator.

1. Building Scales

Most well constructed questionnaires will be structured to include scales that are composed of a number of individual questionnaire items. Any one question in a survey may do an inadequate job of measuring a variable or a concept. Therefore many surveys include multiple questions relating to the same concept. Those questions can then be combined into a general measure of the concept (sometimes called a scale). An example of a scale is the group goal-clarity scale from the Michigan Assessment of Organizations questionnaire (Survey Research Center, 1975). It is composed of three questionnaire items and respondents express agreement or disagreement with each using a 7-point Likert-type response format. The items are as follows:

Group goal clarity
My group knows exactly what things it has to get done.

Each member of my work group has a clear idea of the group's goals.

In my work group we can generally tell what has to be done next.

These three questions all measure part of the larger concept of the clarity of the goals that a work group has. Using only one of these questions would give only a partial measurement of the whole concept. By using three questions to measure the concept, several advantages are realized. First, the concept is measured more completely since several dimensions rather than just one dimension are measured. Second, the total measure, if constructed well, is accurate. While a person might make a mistake or respond incorrectly to one question, it is doubtful that such a mistake would occur over three such items, spread over different parts of a questionnaire. Third, the multiple item scale permits "quality control" of the questionnaire. The responses of the same person on one question should be similar to responses on other questions (the items should be correlated) if the questionnaire is reliable.

Given that many questionnaires include scales, an early step in analysis is to aggregate responses to individual questions into scales. Aggregation is usually done in one of two ways. First, for each respondent, the scores on the different items (in this case, the three goal-clarity questions) can be added to get a total scale score. Another approach that is used frequently is to get a mean (an arithmetic average of the three scores) across the items. In this case, the mean would give a number in the 1 to 7 range.

By computing scale scores, the analyst reduces the number of different numbers that he or she has to work with in further analysis. The scale scores, representing multiple responses related to a concept rather than responses to one specific question, may be both more meaningful and more reliable than a single item score.

At the same time, there are occasions when the scale score has some disadvantages. One of these situations is during feedback, where having scales requires explanation of the scaling procedure. It is frequently easier for people to understand the meaning of a set of responses to a specific question than to understand the meaning of an aggregated scale score.

In summary, the analyst will probably want to construct scales, but he or she may also want to continue to work with some of the individual items. In addition, some specially constructed items may not fall into preset scales. Both scales and item scores are useful in different ways. The next steps of analysis are equally applicable to scale scores.

2. Obtaining Means Across Respondents

The next step is to summarize the responses of a number of people, either for an item or a scale. One way of summarizing many responses is to calculate a mean (arithmetic average) of the responses of different individuals to the same question. For example, consider the following questionnaire item:

All in all, how satisfied are you with your job?

(1) Very dissatisfied

(2) Dissatisfied

(3) Neither satisfied nor dissatisfied

(4) Satisfied

(5) Very satisfied

Suppose this were used in a questionnaire given to 200 people in an organization: 50 people checked the (3) response; 100 people checked the (4) response; and 50 people checked the (5) response. We could summarize by adding up the value of all the responses (the frequency of one response multiplied by its numerical value) and dividing by the number of people responding:

A.   50 people checking the 3 response = 150
     100 people checking the 4 response = 400
      50 people checking the 5 response = 250
     ———
                             Total = 800

B. $\dfrac{800 \text{ (sum of frequencies times response values)}}{200 \text{ (total number of respondents)}} = 4.0 \text{ (mean)}$

The mean of 4.0 is a summary figure, describing the responses of the 200 people to this question. The mean is a useful summary point. It is economical in that it summarizes much data in a single number. The responses of a large number of people to a large number of questions can easily be summarized in the listing of means for questionnaire items. The mean has a quantitative value so that it can be compared to other numbers (such as means on other questions or other scales, means from other administrations of the questionnaire, or means of other people's responses).

On the other hand, the mean also has disadvantages. It gives up descriptive power in return for the ability to summarize. Therefore other summary measures also should be used to look at the data.

3. Plotting Frequency Distributions

One of the basic problems of the mean is that different configurations of responses can result in the same score. Thinking about the same question (satisfaction) used above, look at the following sets of data from two different samples:

Question: All in all, how satisfied are you with your job?

Sample 1		
Response	*Number checking each response*	*Graph**
(1)	0	
(2)	0	
(3)	50	XXXXX
(4)	100	XXXXXXXXXX
(5)	50	XXXXX

Sample 2		
Response	*Number checking each response*	*Graph**
(1)	30	XXX
(2)	20	XX
(3)	0	
(4)	20	XX
(5)	130	XXXXXXXXXXXXX

*Each X = 10 people checking the response.

In both of these samples the mean is 4.0, but obviously, one would not interpret the responses in both cases as having the same implications.

A second technique, which accounts for this problem is the frequency distribution. As shown for sample 1 and sample 2 above, one can list (and even graphically display) the number (frequency) of people who checked each of the five alternative answers. The distribution of the answers thus provides a more detailed summary of how a number of different people answered a question. While not having the easy comparability of the mean score, it does provide more information and during feedback may be more meaningful to organizational members than the simple listing of a single average number.

4. *Comparison to Standards*

Once means and frequency distributions have been obtained, the analyst in an organization often faces another problem. If, as in the first example the mean response is 4.0, is a 4.0 good or bad? In short, what does a 4.0 signify?

The only way that the 4.0 can have more than the most general meaning is to compare it with some other score. What many find useful is to compare the score to some kind of standard that will help the members of the organization as well as the consultant come to a judgment as to whether the score is "good" or "bad." Frequently, standards for comparison are obtained by looking at the responses of large numbers of people to the same question. For example, some standardized surveys have been used in a number of different organizations and those who distribute the survey have on file the responses of thousands of individuals to each of the questions. The mean or frequency distribution of these thousands of responses provides one possible comparison point. Similarly, some of these "data banks" have the capacity of generating comparison scores for a specific subgroup, such as those people who are in industries similar to the one being surveyed or from a similar part of the country, or similar kinds of employees (i.e., white collar, blue collar, managerial, etc.). It is important, however, to identify a comparison group that is meaningful for the particular organization that has been surveyed.

Perhaps the most appropriate comparison group is the organization itself. Once a questionnaire has been administered, future administrations can be compared to earlier administrations. Thus means and distributions can be compared to means and distributions of the same organization at an earlier time.

5. Comparisons Within the Organization

Another kind of comparison that may provide useful information is the comparison within the organization—looking at data from different groups or parts of the organization in relation to each other. For example, means and distributions might be compared for different levels of the organizational hierarchy, for different work groups, for different departments or divisions, for union vs. non-union employees, for hourly vs. exempt employees, etc. These comparisons, particularly when combined with a diagnostic model that can be used to interpret the implications of the comparisons, can be particularly useful.

6. Other Techniques

There are obviously a host of other techniques. For example, techniques exist to test whether the differences of scores between groups are indeed real and significant rather than illusory or due to chance (t-tests and analysis of variance, for example) and other techniques can be used to look at the relationships between different items and scales (correlation, multiple regression, etc.). These will not be discussed in detail, but the practitioner should be aware that they exist. The procedures discussed here are only the most elementary techniques that can be used. They do, however, serve the purpose of helping to summarize, understand, and ask questions of a set of data that has been collected.

SOURCES OF TECHNICAL EXPERTISE

There are many times when people in organizations may not be able to conduct their own data analysis due to a lack of either expertise or facilities to do adequate technical analysis. For example, the absence of a computer facility would make it extremely difficult to do even the simple analyses described above if the sample size were very large. In addition, there may be a need to do more sophisticated analysis than the kind outlined above. In these cases, other sources of technical expertise need to be identified. A few of the most common sources are as follows.

The Consultant

An obvious source of expertise is the consultant. Many consultants have training in statistical analysis and have access to computer facilities to work with the data that are collected. In general, having a consultant who is competent in data analysis is a desirable thing. There is one minor danger, however, when the consultant does the analysis. If the internal partners are not comfortable with quantitative analysis, the process of analysis may be one of the consultant ''going away'' to use secret formulae and strange tools only to reappear with camera-ready charts and diagrams. The danger is that the internal partners may not continue to truly be partners with the consultant and may lose some sense of ownership over the data. The consultant needs to work collaboratively with the members of the organization so that they understand, at least intuitively, what he is doing with the data.

Another External Resource

If the consultant does not have the specific skills or facilities, other external sources of expertise can be identified. For example, the consultant might be asked to contact another consultant who has those skills to aid him or her in the analysis. Some frequently used resources are the graduate departments of universities, where graduate students and sometimes faculty may be willing to aid in the analysis process.

Internal Resources

Organizational members frequently forget the kinds of resources that exist within the organization itself. There frequently are people within the organization who have the expertise to do data analysis, who usually apply that expertise to different kinds of problems. A primary example is a market research department that works with data (and frequently survey data) and can easily perform the technical parts of analysis. Other groups, such as management science/analysis groups, data processing, etc., may also be sources of such expertise.

Prepackaged Analysis

In some cases, standardized questionnaires can be purchased along with preconstructed and prepackaged analysis of the results. In these cases the organization buys not only the questionnaire, but the service of summarizing the data, subjecting the data to certain statistical tests, and producing readable summary and feedback reports. This obviously can save a good deal of time and effort in the organization. At the same time, there are drawbacks to the prepackaged analysis. First, it requires use of a standardized questionnaire, and problems with standardized questionnaires were discussed earlier. Second, when one buys such a service, one frequently is also buying the underlying conceptual model that guides the questionnaire construction and analysis. The importance of that choice is not always obvious. The underlying model and rationale for the questionnaire and the analysis procedure should be examined carefully by both the consultant and the internal partners.

SUMMARY

Data analysis and interpretation are obviously an important part of the data-collection/feedback cycle. Inaccurate or inadequate analysis can send a data feedback effort off into fruitless and erroneous directions. It's therefore important to do analysis competently. It's also important to remember that analysis has two elements. Knowing what questions to ask of the data that has been collected is as important as (and perhaps more important than) the specific techniques of asking those questions.

APPENDIX B
SAMPLES OF INSTRUMENTS

A few data-collection instruments have been included here as illustrations of some of the approaches and methods used to collect data in organizations. Specifically, the following instruments are included:

1. *Orientation Interview*: A structured, open-ended interview guide used to do preliminary data gathering in an organization.

2. *Short Form Questionnaire*: The questionnaire used in the PNB case to collect data from employees of bank branches on a monthly basis.

3. *Group Effectiveness Survey*: A survey used to collect data on certain aspects of group functioning. Includes questionnaire items in different forms.

4. *Feedback form for group effectiveness survey*: One version of a computer generated report for feeding back the results of the group effectiveness survey to a work group.

GENERAL ORIENTATION INTERVIEW

Instructions: This interview guide is designed to be used for preliminary data collection in an organization. Included are a list of open-ended questions that can be used to conduct an interview, that could last from 20 minutes to 2 hours. Such an interview usually will be used after the consultant has entered the organization and made introductory presentations to employees. The questions are to be used as a general guide, rather than as a script which must be adhered to strictly. In most sections of the interview there is a beginning question, followed by one or more questions designed to follow up on the main question and to probe for additional information. These follow-up/probe questions are optional.

Introduction to Interviewee:

Hello, my name is _____.
I was here not long ago to describe a project that I am working on in this organization. (Review basic goals of specific OD program, and answer any questions that the interviewee may have about the project before proceeding further.)

As I mentioned the last time I was here, one of the first things that I have to do is to learn about this organization and what it's like to work here. One way of doing this is to interview some of the people who work here. I have asked to speak to people working at different levels and in different work units. Specific individuals were picked at random, essentially like picking a name out of a hat. Your name was picked as one of the people to be interviewed from this unit.

What I would like to do is to spend about an hour today talking with you about your job, this organization, and how things are around here. I have a set of questions that I will be asking you. These are basically the same questions that everyone who is interviewed will be asked. Some of these questions will seem a little vague, but please answer the questions based on what you think they mean. If you don't know the answer or don't feel like talking about a topic, let me know and we will move on to the next set of questions.

A final note; during this interview I'd like you to be as open and frank as you can. The contents of this interview are *strictly confidential*. No one except you and me will ever know what specifically was said here. I will, of course, be using the information you give me as I begin to work with people here in this organization, but all of the information will be used only in summarized form. No person's individual comments will be seen and no information will be presented in a way that might allow someone to figure out who said what. Before we start, do you have any questions? (Stop for questions.)

As we proceed, I'd like to make some notes so that I can remember what you've said. Do you mind my taking notes? (Stop to make sure.)

Interviewee_____

Date of Interview _____

Location of Interview _____

Interviewer_____

I. THE PERSON AND HIS/HER JOB

A. What is your job title here in this organization?

B. If you had to describe your job to someone who is not familiar with this kind of work, how would you describe what you do?

C. When did you first start working on this job?

D. How long have you worked for this organization?

E. What other jobs have you had in this organization?

II. THE WORK

A. *Main question*: How does the work get done in this unit (department, organization, etc.)?

B. *Probe/follow-up questions*:

   1. How does your job fit into getting the work done?

2. Who do you have to talk with in order to get your work done?

3. What kinds of communication (such as reports, memos, instructions, etc.) do you receive or send out as part of your job?

4. What are the major problems in getting the work done here?

III. GROUPS

A. *Main question*: Could you describe some of the groups that exist here (both formal and informal)?

B. *Probe/follow-up questions*:

1. What kinds of people belong to these groups?

2. How well do these groups get the work done?

3. How do these groups get along with each other?

4. Do you feel as if you are a part of your group?

5. How are decisions made in your group?

6. If you worked particularly well, how would the members of your group feel about you?

IV. SUPERVISION

A. *Main question*: Who is your supervisor (the person who directs your work, gives you assignments, evaluates you, etc.)?

B. *Probe/follow-up questions*:

1. How frequently do you communicate with your supervisor?

2. What kinds of things does your supervisor do to help you do your job?

3. In general, how much say do you have in the decisions that your supervisor makes?

4. In general, how well do you get along with your supervisor.

V. REWARDS

A. *Main question:* If you do a good job, will you get rewarded for it (by pay, promotion, praise, etc.)?

B. *Probe/follow-up questions:*
   1. How is pay determined in this organization?
   2. How are promotions made in this organization?

VI. SATISFACTION

A. *Main Question:* In general, how satisfied are you with working here?

B. *Probe/follow-up questions:*
   1. What things make you most dissatisfied?
   2. What are the things that make you feel most satisfied at work?

VII. PROBLEMS AND CHANGES

A. *Main question:* If you could make any change you wanted in this organization (within reason), what would you change and why?

B. *Probe/follow-up questions:*
   1. What do you see as the major problems in this organization?
   2. What do you see as the major strengths of this organization?
   3. What do you see as the major thing blocking needed changes here?

VIII. UNION ACTIVITY (optional; should be asked earlier in the interview if used)

A. *Main question:* Could you describe the situation here between management and the union(s)?

B. *Probe/follow-up questions:*
   1. Are you a union member? If so, what union?
   2. What do you think of labor-management relations here?
   3. How does the union affect the way you do your job?

Summary:

I've asked you a number of questions about yourself and the organization. Are there other things that I should know about if I want to understand what goes on around here? (Stop, if necessary.)

We've spent some time answering my questions. Do you have any questions that you'd like to ask me? (Stop, if necessary.)

Thank you very much for your help. The information you have provided will be very valuable as we begin trying to understand this organization and begin to work on making it a better place to be. I appreciate your cooperation.

ISR   MONTHLY ATTITUDES FEEDBACK QUESTIONNAIRE

Instructions: This questionnaire is being used to collect data as part of the on-going feedback project of _____ and the Institute for Social Research (ISR) at the University of Michigan. Your branch will be receiving a summary of the responses of all the employees in the branch within a few weeks. No individual data will be fed back and your individual responses will be strictly confidential. Please answer each question as frankly and openly as possible. Do not put your name on this questionnaire.

PLEASE FILL IN THE FOLLOWING IDENTIFICATION INFORMATION:

Branch (Cost Center) Number

Form Number 0   88:01

88:02-04

Your position within the branch:

[1] Teller   88:05

[2] Desk

[3] Management (includes Teller-supervisors, Branch Managers, and Assistant Managers)

Are you: [1] Part time   [2] Full time   88:06

Date: Indicate the month that feedback covers (if distributed in first few days of new month, please record the previous month)

Month Number _____ Year _____   88:07-10

THE FOLLOWING ARE SOME STATEMENTS ABOUT YOU AND YOUR JOB. PLEASE CHECK THE NUMBER THAT INDICATES HOW MUCH YOU AGREE OR DISAGREE WITH EACH STATEMENT. PLEASE READ EACH STATEMENT CAREFULLY.

Strongly Disagree / Disagree / Slightly Disagree / Neither Agree nor Disagree / Slightly Agree / Agree / Strongly Agree

1. It is easy to get other people in this branch to help me when I need it. .... [1] [2] [3] [4] [5] [6] [7]   88:11
2. I get a feeling of personal satisfaction from doing my job well. .... [1] [2] [3] [4] [5] [6] [7]   88:12
3. Decisions in this branch are frequently made without asking the people who have to live with them. .... [1] [2] [3] [4] [5] [6] [7]   88:13
4. The bank rewards those who do their jobs well .... [1] [2] [3] [4] [5] [6] [7]   88:14
5. Communication in this branch is good. .... [1] [2] [3] [4] [5] [6] [7]   88:15
6. I look forward to being with the people in my branch most days. .... [1] [2] [3] [4] [5] [6] [7]   88:16
7. In the next few months, I am likely to look for a job outside of _____ .... [1] [2] [3] [4] [5] [6] [7]   88:17
8. What happens in this branch is really important to me. .... [1] [2] [3] [4] [5] [6] [7]   88:18
9. Each person in this branch has a clear idea of the branch's goals and objectives. .... [1] [2] [3] [4] [5] [6] [7]   88:19
10. All in all, I am satisfied with my job. .... [1] [2] [3] [4] [5] [6] [7]   88:20

PLEASE TURN SHEET OVER AND COMPLETE THE OTHER SIDE

- 2 -

THE FOLLOWING QUESTIONS ASK ABOUT THE QUALITY OF SUPERVISION IN THIS BRANCH. THE STATEMENTS SHOULD BE THOUGHT OF AS REFERRING TO ALL OF THE PEOPLE WHO SUPERVISE OR DIRECT YOUR WORK (THIS COULD INCLUDE TELLER-SUPERVISORS, PEOPLE FUNCTIONING AS ASSISTANT MANAGERS, AND BRANCH MANAGERS). FOR EACH STATEMENT, CHECK THE NUMBER WHICH INDICATES HOW MUCH YOU AGREE OR DISAGREE WITH THE STATEMENT, KEEPING IN MIND ALL OF THE PEOPLE THAT SUPERVISE YOU.

MY SUPERVISORS . . .

Strongly Disagree, Disagree, Slightly Disagree, Neither Agree nor Disagree, Slightly Agree, Agree, Strongly Agree

11. . . . help me solve work related problems. .... [1] [2] [3] [4] [5] [6] [7]   88:21
12. . . . do a good job of planning and scheduling
    working in advance. .... [1] [2] [3] [4] [5] [6] [7]   88:22
13. . . . let me know how well I am doing. .... [1] [2] [3] [4] [5] [6] [7]   88:23
14. . . . are concerned about me as an individual. .... [1] [2] [3] [4] [5] [6] [7]   88:24
15. . . . help subordinates to develop their skills. .... [1] [2] [3] [4] [5] [6] [7]   88:25
16. . . . encourage subordinates to participate in
    important decisions that concern them. .... [1] [2] [3] [4] [5] [6] [7]   88:26

PLEASE ANSWER THE FOLLOWING QUESTION, KEEPING IN MIND THE AREA OR PART OF THE BRANCH IN WHICH YOU WORK MOST OF THE TIME:

17. During the past month, the quality of customer service we have given has been: 88:27

    [1]   [2]   [3]   [4]   [5]   [6]   [7]

    Poor   Average   Excellent

18. PLEASE WRITE IN YOUR UNIVERSITY OF MICHIGAN IDENTIFICATION NUMBER
    IN THIS SPACE: [ ][ ][ ]   88:28-30

    THIS INFORMATION IS IMPORTANT FOR THE SCIENTIFIC WORK IN THIS STUDY.
    NO ONE IN THE BANK HAS ACCESS TO THE LIST OF I D. NUMBERS AND NAMES.
    IF YOU SHOULD MISPLACE YOUR I D. NUMBER PLEASE CALL THE FOLLOWING
    PHONE NUMBER (COLLECT) AT THE UNIVERSITY OF MICHIGAN AND IDENTIFY
    YOURSELF AS A _____ BANK RESPONDENT.

    AREA CODE 313   764-9397

19. (This space is for additional questions which may
    be asked from time to time. If an additional
    question is attached, write in your answer here;
    if no question is attached, ignore this space.)   [1] [2] [3] [4] [5] [6] [7]   88:31

GROUP EFFECTIVENESS SURVEY

(8888)	1:01-04
(blank)	1:05
Group number/letter _____	1:06-07
Date _____ / _____ / _____ mo day yr	1:08-13

Instructions

This survey is designed to collect information on the functioning of your group. As you read the questions, think about how your group has been working and check the response that you feel is most appropriate.

Many of the questions ask about things that "group members" do. Obviously different people act in different ways. Therefore, when answering the questions, think about how group members have behaved in <u>general</u> during the period that you have been working together.

Your individual responses will be confidential. Any feedback of these results will be of aggregated group data.

The Group Task and Composition

1. In general, to what degree are group tasks <u>certain</u> and <u>predictable</u>?   1:14

  The group tasks are very   [1] [2] [3] [4] [5] [6] [7]   The group tasks are very
  unpredictable; we never   predictable; we always
  know what we're going to   know exactly what we are
  have to do next   going to have to do next

2. In general, how <u>complex</u> are the tasks the group has to do?   1:15

  Very simple; most of the   [1] [2] [3] [4] [5] [6] [7]   Very complex; most of the
  work does not require   work requires advanced
  advanced skills, abilities   skills, abilities, or knowledge
  or knowledge

3. How <u>interdependent</u> are the different parts of the group's task?   1:16

  Very independent; each part [1] [2] [3] [4] [5] [6] [7]   Very interdependent; each
  of the task can be done   part of the task is highly
  independently of other   related to other parts of
  parts   the task. Getting one part
                                                                     done is dependent on having
                                                                     other parts done

4. Do group members have the appropriate skills, abilities, and knowledge to do the task?   1:17

  No, members do not have   [1] [2] [3] [4] [5] [6] [7]   Yes, members do have
  skills, abilities, and/or   skills, abilities, and/or
  knowledge needed to do   knowledge needed to do
  the task   the task

How the Group Members Work Together

5. Do most members seem to feel like they are really a part of the group?   1:18

    No, most members do not   [1] [2] [3] [4] [5] [6] [7]   Yes, most members do
    feel a part of the group   feel a part of the group

6. Do all group members appear to be involved in the activities of the group?   1:19

    No, most members don't   [1] [2] [3] [4] [5] [6] [7]   Yes, most members are
    seem to care what happens   very concerned about
    with the group   the group

7. How clear are the goals of the group?   1:20

    Unclear. The group is not   [1] [2] [3] [4] [5] [6] [7]   Clear. The group knows
    sure what it is supposed   exactly what it is supposed
    to do   to do

8. Is there general agreement with the goals of the group?   1:21

    No, different people have   [1] [2] [3] [4] [5] [6] [7]   Yes, everyone shares the
    very different goals for   goals for the group
    the group

9. How even is participation by members?   1:22

    Uneven; a small number of   [1] [2] [3] [4] [5] [6] [7]   Even; everyone talks about
    people do all of the talking   the same amount

10. Do everyone's opinions get listened to?   1:23

    No, many members'   [1] [2] [3] [4] [5] [6] [7]   Yes, all members seem to
    comments are ignored   be listened to by others

11. How open are group members in expressing their feelings in the group?   1:24

    Group members are very   [1] [2] [3] [4] [5] [6] [7]   Group members are very
    closed, guarded, do not   open and express their
    express feelings   feelings freely

12. How supportive are group members toward each other?   1:25

    Not supportive at all   [1] [2] [3] [4] [5] [6] [7]   Very supportive

13. Are group members willing to confront each other or to respond negatively to others?   1:26

    Group members do not   [1] [2] [3] [4] [5] [6] [7]   Group members are very
    confror   confronting

14. How well do members receive negative comments?   1:27

    Poorly; people seem   [1] [2] [3] [4] [5] [6] [7]   Well; people listen to,
    threatened by negative   value, and make use of
    comments and react   negative comments
    defensively

15. How much conflict is expressed in the group?   1:28

Little conflict; the group   [1] [2] [3] [4] [5] [6] [7]   Much conflict; the group
rarely has conflicts expressed   is constantly dealing with
conflicts among members

16. In general, how is conflict dealt with?   (check only one)   1:29

[1] Forcing (person with power wins)
[2] Smoothing (denial of the conflict)
[3] Withdrawal (by one side or member)
[4] Confrontation (those in conflict directly work it out)
[5] Arbitration (a third party decides)
[6] Other _____

17. Are leadership roles and assignments clear?   1:30

No, it's not clear who is   [1] [2] [3] [4] [5] [6] [7]   Yes, it is very clear who
supposed to do what; who   has what leadership
is in charge, etc.   responsibility

18. How much is leadership shared?   1:31

Little; one person does all   [1] [2] [3] [4] [5] [6] [7]   Much; each person performs
of the leadership functions   different leadership functions
as appropriate

19. In general, how effective has the formal leader(s) been in getting the group to work effectively?   1:32

Ineffective; the leader(s) have   [1] [2] [3] [4] [5] [6] [7]   Effective; the leader(s) have
not helped the group to   greatly aided the group in
work effectively   working effectively

20. How much do group members participate in decision making?   1:33

Very little; a few people   [1] [2] [3] [4] [5] [6] [7]   A great deal; the whole
make the decisions while   group is involved in
others are not involved   making most decisions

21. When faced with a task (or a problem to solve) does the group usually plan how it will work
on the task ahead of time (i.e., before beginning to work on it)?   1:34

Usually not; the group tends   [1] [2] [3] [4] [5] [6] [7]   Usually yes; the group tends
to jump right into doing   to discuss how it will do the
the task, rather than dis—   work before starting
cussing how it will be done
first

22. After the group has done work, does the group spend any time discussing how well group
members worked together?   1:35

Usually not   [1] [2] [3] [4] [5] [6] [7]   Yes, frequently

Assessing Group Effectiveness

23. How effective would you rate the group along the following dimensions?

		Ineffective						Effective	
[1]	Problem solving	[1]	[2]	[3]	[4]	[5]	[6]	[7]	1:36
[2]	Making decisions	[1]	[2]	[3]	[4]	[5]	[6]	[7]	1:37
[3]	Getting the work done	[1]	[2]	[3]	[4]	[5]	[6]	[7]	1:38
[4]	Making use of member skills, abilities, resources	[1]	[2]	[3]	[4]	[5]	[6]	[7]	1:39
[5]	Meeting individual needs	[1]	[2]	[3]	[4]	[5]	[6]	[7]	1:40

24. All in all, how satisfied are you with being a member of this group?   1:41

Very dissatisfied   [1]   [2]   [3]   [4]   [5]   [6]   [7]   Very satisfied

25. Overall, how effective is this group?   1:42

Ineffective   [1]   [2]   [3]   [4]   [5]   [6]   [7]   Effective

Strengths and Weaknesses of the Group

Briefly list the major strengths of this group (what things about the group members and how they work together help the group to work well?)

Briefly list the major weaknesses of this group (what things about the group members and how they work together get in the way of the group doing its job?)

8 PEOPLE IN 2 GROUPS COMPLETED THE SURVEY THIS ADMINISTRATION

4 PEOPLE IN YOUR GROUP SUBMITTED A COMPLETED QUESTIONNAIRE

	GROUP MEAN	GROUP STANDARD DEVIATION	MEAN OF ALL 2 GROUPS

THE GROUP TASK AND COMPOSITION

		GROUP MEAN	GROUP STANDARD DEVIATION	MEAN OF ALL 2 GROUPS
1	TASK CERTAINTY	5	1.41421	4.875
2	TASK COMPLEXITY	5.25	.829156	4.875
3	INTERDEPENDENCE	5.5	.866025	5.375
4	MEMBER SKILLS	5.25	.829156	5

HOW THE GROUP MEMBERS WORK TOGETHER

5	MEMBERS FEEL PART OF GRP	5.25	1.08972	4.5
6	MEMBERS INVOLVED IN GRP	5.25	.829156	4.375
7	GROUP GOAL CLARITY	5	1.22474	4.5
8	AGREEMENT ON GOALS	5	1	4.75
9	PARTICIPATION EVEN	4.75	.829156	4.625
10	EVERYONE LISTENED TO	4.75	.829156	4.5
11	OPEN EXPRESSION FEELINGS	5.75	1.08972	5.25
12	SUPPORTIVE TO EACH OTHER	5.5	.866025	5.125
13	CONFRONT EACH OTHER	5.25	.829156	4.75
14	NEG COMMENTS TAKEN WELL	5.75	1.08972	5.375
15	HOW MUCH CONFLICT	5.5	.866025	5.5
16	HOW DEAL W/CONFLICT			
17	LEADERSHIP ROLES CLEAR	4.75	.829156	5.125
18	LEADERSHIP SHARED	5.25	.829156	5.625
19	LEADERSHIP EFFECTIVE	5.25	.829156	5.375
20	PARTICIPATION/DECISIONS	5.75	.829156	5.375
21	PLANNING AHEAD OF TIME	5.25	.829156	5.25
22	DISCUSS GROUP AFTERWARDS	5.25	.433013	5.125

GROUP EFFECTIVENESS

23.1	PROBLEM-SOLVING	5.75	.433013	5.5
23.2	DECISION-MAKING	6	1	5.375
23.2	GETTING WORK DONE	5.5	1.11803	5.375
23.4	USING MEMBER RESOURCES	5.5	.866025	5.375
23.5	MEETING MEMBER NEEDS	6	.707107	5.375
24	HOW SATISFIED W/ GROUP	6	1	5.25
25	OVERALL EFFECTIVENESS	5.5	1.11803	5.25

RESPONSES TO QUESTION 16 --

RESPONSE CODES: _1_ _2_ _3_ _4_ _5_ _6_ _7_

RESPONSES: 2   1   1

THIS ANALYSIS PROGRAM WAS WRITTEN BY SARAH CHARLES AND WEBSTER HULL,
2/77

BIBLIOGRAPHY

Alderfer, C. P. Organizational diagnosis from initial client reactions to a researcher. *Human Organization,* 1968, **27**:260–265.

_____*Improving Organizational Communication Through Long-term Intergroup Intervention* (Technical Report #8). New Haven: Yale University School of Organization and Management, 1975.

Alderfer, C. P., and Brown, L. D. Questionnaire design in organizational research. *J. of Applied Psychology,* 1972, **56**:456–460.

Alderfer, C. P., and Ferris R. Understanding the impact of survey feedback. In W. W. Burke and H. A. Hornstein (Eds.). *The Social Technology of Organization Development.* Fairfax, Va.: NTL Learning Resources Corp., 1972, pp. 234–243.

Alderfer, C. P., and Holbrook, J. A new design for survey feedback. *Education and Urban Society,* 1973, **5**:437–464.

Ammons, R. B. Effects of knowledge of performance: A survey and tentative theoretical formulation. *J. of General Psychology,* 1956, **54**:279–299.

Annett, J. *Feedback and Human Behavior: The Effects of Knowledge of Results, Incentives and Reinforcement on Learning and Performance.* Baltimore: Penguin Books, 1969.

Argyris, C. Diagnosing defenses against the outsider. *J. Social Issues.* 1952, **8**(3):24–32.

_____*Intervention Theory and Method.* Reading, Mass.: Addison-Wesley, 1970.

Bales, R. F. *Personality and Interpersonal Behavior.* New York: Holt, Rinehart, Winston, 1971.

Baumgartel, H. Using employee questionnaire results for improving organizations: The survey "feedback" experiment. *Kansas Business Review,* 1959, **12**(12):2–6.

Beckhard, R., *Organization Development: Strategies and Models.* Reading Mass.: Addison-Wesley, 1969.

Bennis, W. G. *Organization Development: Its Nature, Origins, and Prospects.* Reading, Mass.: Addison-Wesley, 1969.

Bennis, W. G.; Berlew, D. E.; Schein, E. H.; and Steele, F. I. *Interpersonal Dynamics: Essays and Readings on Human Interaction.* Homewood, Ill.: Dorsey Press, 1973.

Bouchard, T. J., Jr. Field research methods: Interviewing, questionnaires, participant observation, unobtrusive measures. In M. D. Dunnette (Ed.) *Handbook of Industrial and Organizational Psychology.* Chicago: Rand McNally, 1976, p. 363–413.

Bowers, D. G. OD techniques and their results in 23 organizations: The Michigan ICL Study. *J. of Applied Behavioral Science,* 1973, **9**:21–43.

Bowers, D. G., and Franklin, J. L. Survey-guided development: Using human resources measurement in organizational change. *J. of Contemporary Business,* 1972, **1**:43–55.

———*Survey-guided Development: Data Based Organizational Change.* Ann Arbor: Institute for Social Research, 1976.

Brown, L. D. "Research action": Organizational feedback understanding, and change. *J. of Applied Behavioral Science,* 1972, **8**:697–711.

Callahan, D. M., and Lake, D. G. Changing a community college. *Education and Urban Society.* 1973, **6**:22–48.

Cammann, C. *The impact of a feedback system on managerial attitudes and performance.* (Unpublished doctoral dissertation). Yale University, 1974.

Cammann, C., and Nadler, D. A. Fit control systems to your management style. *Harvard Business Review,* 1976, **54**(1):65–72.

Chesler, M., and Flanders, M. Resistance to research and research utilization: The death and life of a feedback attempt. *J. of Applied Behavioral Science,* 1967, **4**:469–487.

Coughlan, R. J., and Cooke, R. A. *The Structural Development of Educational Organizations.* Ann Arbor: Survey Research Center, 1974.

Galbraith, J. R. *Designing Complex Organizations.* Reading, Mass.: Addison-Wesley, 1973.

Hackman, J. R., and Oldham, G. R. Development of the job diagnostic survey. *J. of Applied Psychology,* 1975, **60**:159–170.

Hausser, D. L.; Pecorella, P. A.; and Wissler, A. L. *Survey-guided Development: A Manual for Consultants,* Ann Arbor: Institute for Social Research, 1975.

Hays, W. L. *Statistics.* New York: Holt, Rinehart, and Winston, 1963.

Heller, F. A. Group feedback analysis as a change agent. *Human Relations,* 1970, **23**:319–333.

International Business Machines. *Manager's Guide: The Opinion Survey.* (Internal company publication). Armonk, New York: IBM, 1974.

Jenkins, G. D.; Nadler, D. A.; Lawler, E. E.; and Cammann, C. Standardized observations: An approach to measuring the nature of jobs. *J. of Applied Psychology,* 1975, **60**:171–181.

Kahn, R. L., and Cannell, C. F. *The Dynamics of Interviewing.* New York: Wiley, 1967.

Katz, D., and Kahn, R. L. *The Social Psychology of Organizations.* New York: Wiley, 1966.

Klein, S. M.; Kraut, A. I.; and Wolfson, A. Employee reactions to attitude survey feedback: A study of the impact of structure and process. *Administrative Science Quarterly,* 1971, **16**:497–514.

Kolb, D. A., and Frohman, A. L. An organization development approach to consulting. *Sloan Management Review,* 1970, **12**:51–65.

Lawler, E. E. *Motivation in Work Organizations.* Belmont, California: Brooks/Cole, 1973.

Lawler, E. E., and Rhode, J. G. *Information and Control in Organizations.* Santa Monica, Calif.: Goodyear, 1976.

Lawrence, P. R., and Lorsch, J. W. *Developing Organizations: Diagnosis and Action.* Reading, Mass.: Addison-Wesley, 1969.

Levinson, H. *Organizational Diagnosis.* Cambridge: Harvard University Press, 1972.

Likert, R. *New Patterns of Management.* New York: McGraw-Hill, 1961.

_____*The Human Organization: Its Management and Value.* New York: McGraw-Hill, 1967.

Locke, E. A.; Cartledge, N.; and Koeppel, J. Motivational effects of knowledge of results: A goal-setting phenomenon. *Psychological Bulletin,* 1968, **70**:474–485.

Macy, B. A., and Mirvis, P. H. A methodology for assessment of quality of work life and organizational effectiveness in behavioral economic terms. *Administrative Science Quarterly,* 1976, **21**:212–226.

Mann, F. C. Studying and creating change: A means to understanding social organization. In C. M. Arensberg *et al.,* (Eds.). *Research in Industrial Human Relations: A Critical Appraisal.* New York: Harper, 1957.

Mann, F. C., and Likert, R. The need for research on the communication of research results. *Human Organization,* 1952, **11**:15–19.

McCall, G. and Simmons, J. *Issues in Participant Observation.* Reading, Mass.: Addison-Wesley, 1969.

McElvaney, C. T., and Miles, M. B. Using survey feedback in consultation. In R. A. Schmuck and M. B. Miles (Eds.). *Organization Development in Schools.* La Jolla, Calif.: National Press Books, 1971.

Miles, M. B.; Hornstein, H. A.; Callahan, D. M.; Calder, P. H.; and Schiavo, R. S. The consequences of survey feedback: Theory and evaluation. In Bennis, *et al. The Planning of Change.* New York: Holt, Rinehart, and Winston, 1969, pp. 457–468.

Mohrman, A. M., Jr.; Duncan, R. B.; and Cooke, R. A. *A survey feedback organization development program for educational systems.* Paper presented at the meeting of the American Psychological Association, August 1975.

Morris, W. C. and Sashkin, M. *Organization Behavior in Action: Skill Building Experiences.* St. Paul: West, 1976.

Nadler, D. A. Using feedback for organizational change: Promises and pitfalls. *Group and Organization Studies,* 1976, **1**:177–186.

Nadler, D. A.; Mirvis, P. H.; and Cammann, C. The ongoing feedback system: Experimenting with a new managerial tool. *Organizational Dynamics,* 1976, **4**(4):63–80.

Nadler, D. A., and Tushman, M. L. A diagnostic model for organizational behavior. In J. R. Hackman, E. E. Lawler, and L. W. Porter (Eds.) *Perspectives on Behavior in Organizations.* New York: McGraw-Hill, 1977, pp. 85–100.

National Quality of Work Center. *The Quality of Work Program: The First Eighteen Months.* Washington, D. C.: National Quality of Work Center, 1975.

Neff, F. Survey research: A tool for problem diagnosis and improvement in organizations. In A. W. Gouldner and S. M. Miller (Eds.). *Applied Sociology.* New York: Free Press, 1965, pp. 23–38.

Newman, W. H. *Constructive Control: Design and use of control systems.* Englewood Cliffs: Prentice-Hall, 1975.

Nie, N. H.; Hull, C. H.; Jenkins, J. G.; Steinbrenner, K.; and Bent, D. H. *Statistical Package for the Social Sciences* (second edition). New York: McGraw-Hill, 1975.

Nisberg, J. N. Personal communication. May 1976.

Peak, H. Attitude and motivation. In M. R. Jones, (Ed.) *Nebraska Symposium on Motivation.* Lincoln: University of Nebraska Press, 1955, pp. 149–188.

Pettigrew, A. Information control as a power resource. *Sociology,* 1972, **6**:187–204.

Sashkin, M., and Cooke, R. A. *The effects of survey feedback organization development as conditioned by organizational technology and structure.* Paper presented at the National Meeting of the Academy of Management, August 1976.